LIGHT YEAR '87

LIGHT YEAR
'87

Edited by Robert Wallace

With drawings by Jeanne Meinke

Bits Press
Cleveland

The acknowledgments on pages 263-264 constitute a
continuation of this copyright notice.

Associate editors: C. M. Seidler, Bonnie Jacobson.

Printed and bound in the U.S.A.

ISBN: 0-933248-07-5
ISSN: 0743-913X

Light Year, the annual of light verse and funny poems,
welcomes submissions. Poems recently published in
periodicals are OK. SASE, please. To:

> Bits Press
> Department of English
> Case Western Reserve University
> Cleveland, Ohio 44106

811.08
LIG
1987

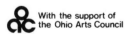 With the support of
the Ohio Arts Council

The Truth must dazzle gradually
Or every man be blind—

> *Emily Dickinson*

The Hen it is a noble beast,
The Cow is more forlorner
Standing in the rain
With a leg at every corner.

> *William McGonagall*
> *(1830-1902)*

CONTENTS

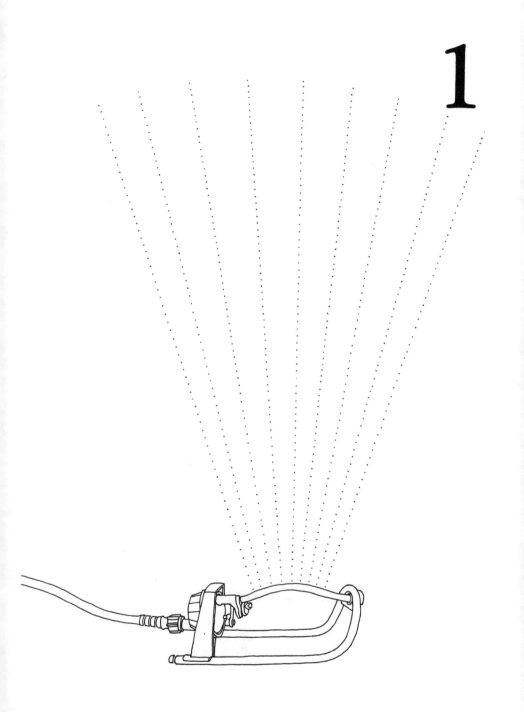

1

MONEY

That money talks
I won't deny.
I heard it once,
It said, "Goodbye."

Richard Armour

POSTCARD FROM CIVILIZATION

We've rented a modern house on a dead-end street
Almost like all the others on the street.
The contract tells us, Keep the garden neat,
And so we try to keep the garden neat.
I haven't the touch that makes a green thing grow,
But I can follow a mower, and I mow.

Piston-like, my Suffolk Colt and I
Range up and down the garden, up and down,
While over hedges, unknown neighbors ply
Like pistons in their gardens, up and down.
Each of us slides within his cylinder;
The engine runs, the City is secure.

E pluribus unum: out of many, one;
Yet independence makes the engine run,
And launched like astronauts we whirl around
These ordered orbits over the common ground,
Achieving our personal visions, high and alone —
O, green and sweet is the smell of the soul new-mown.

Charles W. Pratt

MATERIALISM

Did you think all that stuff you gave me
would make me stay with you?
Well, it helped; and I'm still here,
and I want more stuff.

R. P. Dickey

FINANCIAL NOTE

In living, as in music,
it's clear enough to see:
One cannot get *fa*
without the *do, re, me.*

John D. Engle, Jr.

WHAT'S ALL THIS FUSS ABOUT TAX REFORM?

We know that death and taxes
Are held in wide disfavor;
But why change just the latter?
It's clear the former's graver.

Since it's human to resist
Their power of preemption,
Why not reform the former?
It offers *no* exemption.

If legislation can redress
The cost of what appalls,
Perhaps it's time we opted
For a *pair* of overhauls!

Ned Pastor

SELF EMPLOYMENT

I pick pennies up
off the sidewalk.
It takes one second each.
Sixty seconds, sixty minutes:
thirty-six dollars every hour.

The pay is good but
the work is rather degrading
and there is a long, long wait
between job opportunities.

Lowell E. Sargeant

MAYBE DATS YOUWR PWOBLEM TOO

All my pwoblems
who knows, maybe evwybody's pwoblems
is due to da fact, due to da awful twuth
dat I am SPIDERMAN.

I know, I know. All da dumb jokes:
No flies on you, ha ha,
and da ones about what do I do wit all
doze extwa legs in bed. Well, dat's funny yeah.
But you twy being
SPIDERMAN for a month or two. Go ahead.

You get doze cwazy calls fwom da
Gubbener askin you to twap some booglar who's
only twying to wip off color T.V. sets.
Now, what do I cawre about T.V. sets?
But I pull on da suit, da stinkin suit,
wit da sucker cups on da fingers,
and get my wopes and wittle bundle of
equipment and den I go flying like cwazy
acwoss da town fwom woof top to woof top.

Till der he is. Some poor dumb color T.V. slob
and I fall on him and we westle a widdle
until I get him all woped. So big deal.

You tink when you SPIDERMAN
der's sometin big going to happen to you.
Well, I tell you what. It don't happen dat way.
Nuttin happens. Gubbener calls, I go.
Bwing him to powice. Gubbener calls again,
like dat over and over.

I tink I twy sometin diffunt. I tink I twy
sometin excitin like wacing cawrs. Sometin to make
my heart beat at a difwent wate.
But den you just can't quit being sometin like
SPIDERMAN.
You SPIDERMAN for life. Fowever. I can't even
buin my suit. It won't buin. It's fwame wesistent.
So maybe dat's youwr pwoblem too, who knows.
Maybe dat's da whole pwoblem wif evwytin.
Nobody can buin der suits, day all fwame wesistent.
Who knows?

Jim Hall

SELF HELP

"Big deal. If I could swim as good as him, I'd win a lot
of gold medals, too."
—spectator's comment on Mark Spitz's seventh win
at the 1972 Olympics

Let's get mad, fellow losers, fellow flops,
fellow dust eaters, fellow weepers,
fellow had-a-wife-and-couldn't-keep-hers;
let's get mad and bad and high in the stirrups!
They never liked us, never gave us diddley
when we needed a break. Who the hell are *they*,
anyway? A hundred thousand softies, tops,
moping over their petits fours, worried

that the help these days is getting just too
uppity to lick a boot, or that the snowpack
at Aspen might be, well, simply intolerable.
We're billions strong, tough as dandelions,
raised on humble pie and hind tit;
and we've had a bellyful, up to our eyeballs.

Don't forget: without us, nobody
wins, so let's knock off the oo's
and ah's, the encores, the *Wall Street Journal*.
Let em play the Superbowl to an empty
Superdome, let the election returns read zero
to zero, let em fight the next war
by their lonesomes, with caviar and empty
Mouton Rothchild bottles. Boycott their movies,
their mouthwashes, their douche bags, their life
insurance, their grinning eight-by-ten glossies.

We'll show em what losing's like, put
the boots to em, head em off at the pass, trap em
in a box canyon, take their children hostage
and teach the little snots our primitive ways,
to say "Oh well" and "What's the use" when they
take the wrong turnoff, bobble the punt,
borrow from the guy with the two big friends
named Principal and Interest. Leave em with nothing
to fall back on but a rock and a hard place,
the devil and the deep blue sea, chaos
and old night, aces and eights, Household
Finance and the *Reader's Digest* Sweepstakes. And let
all their letters begin with, "Dear Applicant:
Thank you for letting us see your resumé" or
"Dear Customer: A good credit rating
is a serious responsibility, not a right."

We've got the bench, we've got general admission,
we've got bad stomachs, bad arches, bad
checks, bad timing, bad luck,
bad news, and the worst, the very worst
intentions. Remember "Wrong Way" Corrigan,
General Burgoyne, Harold Stassen, Pickett's
Charge, the electric spaghetti fork, Troy
Donahue, Troy, the Edsel, leisure suits,
Dynaflow, the Maginot Line, and Casey
at the bat, not to mention Uncle Sol
and his worm farm. Let's reach down
for that minus ten percent, that faulty premise,
those visions and revisions, that bush-league,
cockeyed, backfiring, two-left-footed,
shit-for-brains urge to go out there
and do something,
sort of.

William Trowbridge

NIGHT OPERATIONS, COASTAL COMMAND RAF

Remembering that war, I'd near believe
We didn't need the enemy, with whom
Our dark encounters were confused and few
And quickly done, so many of our lot
Did for themselves in folly and misfortune.

Some hit our own barrage balloons, and some
Tripped over power lines, coming in low;
Some swung on takeoff, others overshot,
And two or three forgot to lower the wheels.

There were those that flew the bearing for the course
And flew away forever; and the happy few
That homed on Venus sinking beyond the sea
In fading certitude. For all the skill,
For all the time of training, you might take
The hundred steps in darkness, not the next.

Howard Nemerov

FROM AN ATHLETE LIVING OLD

Since few remember '24
When I won the hundred yard,
My medals are for me alone;
For you, kind sir, my credit card.

James Camp

WHAT'S IN A NAME

Frank, the Animal, Fletcher, face peeled
and running like a tomato about
to be canned; John, the Beast, Mugabi,
gloved fists hammering like twin sledges
in a feature bout, I can understand.
Throw in, for good measure, Bazooka
Limon; James, the Heat, Kinchen; a few
wrestlers (Greg, the Hammer, Valentine;
Junk Yard Dog; Brutus Beefcake; Kamala
with half moons and stars painted all over
his face and shoulders). Who doesn't
enjoy the spectacle of sports? But Carl,
the Truth, Williams? What does he know?
At least Diogenes had a sense of humor.
Can't you just see him with his lantern
at the Cow Palace or Madison Square Garden?
"Hey, man, what's with the dress? And where
you going with that light? You one of those
Moonies or something?" While Carl, the Truth,
Williams tries to beat a fellow boxer's
brains out. There must be poetic justice
somewhere, if only hypothetically, in all this.

Ed Orr

A HISTORY OF GOLF—SORT OF

More than 500 years ago in Scotland, men became
so distracted by the game of golf that they were ne-
glecting archery and other military activities. So, start-
ing in 1457, three successive Scottish kings prohibited
golf. But the fourth king, James IV, became an avid
golfer.

On Scotland's rolling highlands in
    The fifteenth century,
The Scots were playing golf; a change
    From their barbarity.

But not for long. The game was banned
    By three old-fashioned kings.
The Scots returned to archery
    And other warlike things.

Then James the Fourth assumed the throne,
    And he took up the game.
He liked it. As an honor, they
    Immortalized his name.

From tee to green throughout the world,
    Thenceforth and evermore,
When golfers go around the course,
    You'll hear them holler, "IV!"

Thomas L. Hirsch

THE SOMETIME SPORTSMAN
GREETS THE SPRING

When winter's glaze is lifted from the greens,
And cups are cut again, and birdies sing,
Triumphantly the stifled golfer preens
In cleats and slacks once more, and checks his swing.

This year, he vows, his head will steady be,
His weight-shift smooth, his grip and stance ideal;
And so they are, until upon the tee
Befall the old contortions of the real.

So, too, the tennis-player, torpid from
Hibernal months of television sports,
Perfects his serve and feels his knees become
Sheer muscle in their unaccustomed shorts.

Right arm relaxed, the left controls the toss
(Or *vice versa*), and the racket face
Shall at a certain angle sweep across
The floated sphere with gutty strings—an ace!

The mind's eye sees it all until upon
The courts of life the faulty way we played
In other summers rolls back with the sun.
Hope springs eternal; spring hopes, however, fade.

John Updike

QUIDIRON PRO QUO

What happy reciprocity
When golden autumn calls.
For then footballs will fill the air
And air will fill the balls.

Paul Sawyer

THE GIFT

On lines from Emily Dickinson's letters

A one-armed man conveyed the flowers.
I gave him half a smile.

Lewis Turco

IN A STATION OF THE IRT

She said "Good morning" and he said
"That's the way these ugly rumors start."

F. F. Burch

TUESDAY

I like Tuesday.
It's the teenage day of the week.
Still time left
For the week to amount to something.

Alma Denny

AT A CONCERT

They held everything together
as they played, the husband-wife
duo-pianists, famous, getting through
long complicated sonatas and rondos.
This involves them and such excellence.
No, this is about me. Or them.
They played. They were around forty.
Once they were children, practicing
This is what I was thinking.
Once they were children, practicing.
This is what it has all come to.
They played Clementi; the romantics.
This is what it has come to.
This is a life. I knew them. I wept.
Once they were children, practicing.

R. P. Dickey

HELIUM: AN INERT GAS

My ego, like a pink balloon,
    bobs on a string behind
or floats above me where I sit—
    self-effacing, kind.

Sometimes I hug it to my chest
    getting in and out of cars
or ask my friends to hold it for me,
    especially in bars.

My boss says keep it out of sight
     in the kneehole of my desk.
In traffic, how it dances, jerks
     in nervous arabesque!

I should not bring it to the table,
     but when I come, it comes,
though kids giggle and point at it
     and pummel it with crumbs.

Sometimes I dream it drifts away
     above the curling sea,
though it is safely under the sheet
     between my wife and me.

My doctors, friends, and family
     all wonder what's inside.
I think they'd like to pop it, watch
     it flabbily subside.

Judson Jerome

THE PUMPKIN MAN

All summer long and all day long he sits
And fills a chair outside his shanty door.
And now he swats a fly and now he spits
And now is unassertive as before.

In contour, color, general disposition
He comes as near as human nature can
To pumpkinhood—a pumpkin's range, ambition,
Outlook on life. Briefly, a pumpkin man.

Here from my house he looks superbly fed
Though when he eats and what I cannot tell.
If sometime after dark he goes to bed
And sleeps, I think he must sleep very well.

But all day long and summer long he sits
And contemplates poor busy-body me
The way a toad might overtax its wits
Watching the antics of a nervous bee.

Robert Francis

GAS MAN

I am a meter reader
For Connecticut Natural Gas.
I learned to read the meter
In a meter reading class.
I was taught speed meter reading
And when they gave the test,
I was a fleeter meter reader
Than any of the rest.

Now I'm a meter reader leader
And my job is really fun.
I wave a friendly greeting
To the customers I'm meeting,
But don't even stop for eating,
Reading meters while I run.

Pyke Johnson, Jr.

FIELD GUIDE TO NORTH AMERICAN BIRDS

The watchers wade and wait in the water,
half hidden in rushes and cattails,
binoculars aimed at the sky
which is, for the untrained,
a lidless blue, blank and unoccupied.

Bird at 1 o'clock
they cry, as a mote appears,
a speck of brown.
Could it be a crested dowager?
       an olivaceous private?
       a hooded academic?
No, no, it's a northern snitch—
       see the buff rump,
       the dark moustache,
       the spectacles.

We who have no field marks,
who lose the flight patterns
from our scopes
stand dumb in the mud,
no checks on our life lists,
tone deaf to the twitters around us,
the ethereal flutelike tones
of farthingale,
   martinet,
   quark.

Barbara Crooker

EATING OUT

Odd, how from the hum of restaurant noise
One line stood out: "You are what you eat."
I paused, dismissed a thought,
Crunched my final shrimp and gulped it down.
I smelled fried chicken, t-bone steak,
Then glanced to see guys twice my size
Stuff themselves, then moo, or flap their wings.

Gene Fehler

WHAT A FRIEND WE HAVE IN CHEESES!
or SING A SONG OF LIEDERKRANZ

> ("Poets have been mysteriously silent on the subject of cheese."
> —G. K. Chesterton)

What a friend we have in cheeses!
For no food more subtly pleases,
Nor plays so grand a gastronomic part;
Cheese imported—not domestic
For we all get indigestic
From the pasteurizer's Kraft and sodden art.

No poem we shall ever see is
Quite as lovely as a Brie, is,
For "the queen of cheese" is what they call the Brie;
If you pay sufficient money
You will get one nice and runny,
And you'll understand what foods these morsels be!

How we covet all the skills it
Takes in making Chèvre or Tilset,
But if getting basic Pot Cheese is your aim,

Take some simple curds and wheys, a
Bit of rennet—Lo! you've Käese!
(Which is what, in German, is a cheese's name.)

Good lasagna, it's a-gotta
Mozzarella and Ricotta
And a lotta freshly grated Parmesan;
With the latter *any* pasta
Will be eaten up much faster,
For with Parmesan an added charm is on.

Ask your average padrone
What he thinks of Provolone,
And the very word will set his eyes aflame;
Then go ask the bounteous Gina
Her reaction to Fontina—
If you'll raise your gaze you'll see she feels the same.

A Pont-l'Evêque *au point!* What ho!
How our juices all will flow!
But don't touch a Pont-l'Evêque beyond that stage,
For what you'll have, you'll surely find
Is just an over-fragrant rind—
There's no benefit to this *fromage* from age.

Claret, dear, not Coca Cola,
When you're having Gorgonzola—
Be particular to serve the proper wines;
Likewise pick a Beaune, not Coke for
Pointing up a Bleu or Roquefort—
Bless the products of the bovines and the vines!

Ave Gouda! Ave Boursault!
Ave Oka even more so!
Ave Neufchâtel, *Saluto* Port Salut!

And another thing with cheeses—
Every allied prospect pleases—
Ah cheese blintzes! Ah Welsh rabbit! Ah fondue!

And we all know that "Say cheese" is
How a cameraman unfreezes
A subject in a stiff, or shy or dour way;
There's no other food so useful,
So bring on a whole cabooseful
Of the stuff of life! The cheeses of the gourmet!

William Cole

ENGLISH EATS

They eat toad-in-the-hole down in Stow-on-the-Wold.
Oh, they eat it with hideous glee
Whether fresh-made or old, whether tepid or cold,
A la mode, or dissolved in strong tea.

Tepid toad-in-the-hole is a load to eat whole
For its warts rather stick to the tongue,
And you'll find, bless your soul, that cold toad-in-the-hole
May indefinitely stopper your bung.

So take care: Pinch its roll, which must be soft as coal,
Ascertain that your toad's young and spry.
If perchance, doing dirt, it should take aim and squirt,
Be assured that here's mud in your eye.

X. J. Kennedy

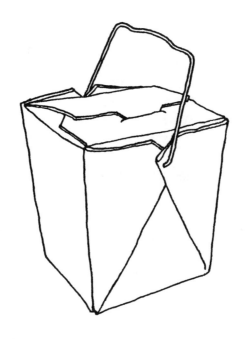

THE TV CHEF

There's a smile upon his face as he adroitly flips and
        tosses
All the complicated sauces from a pan onto a platter.
Then he mixes up the batter to begin the preparation
Of some delicate creation, still with smile upon his face.

With a smile upon his face, he overlooks the dirty dishes,
All the pots and pans, and wishes to his viewers pleasant
        cooking.
No, you never catch him looking at the mess that's left
        for later.
Then you know why the creator wears that smile upon his
        face.

Robert N. Feinstein

RED RASPBERRIES

Velvet thimbles,
Ruby beehives—
Of dusty cells,
With tufted tips
On scrawny hairs—
Pomegranate-
Seeded vaults.
Lucent domes
Crushed to jam
On the palate,
Burgundy
Irrigating
Thirsty buds,
Blooming densely
On the soft,
Fertile plain
Of the tongue.

Gary Selden

MSG

Parsley, sage, rosemary, thyme,
Anise, basil, rind of lime
Are fine, but cannot really rate
With monosodium glutamate.

A hint of mint, a slip of sage
May add a zest you cannot gauge,
But the subtlest savor on your plate
Is monosodium glutamate.

Mace? Tumeric? Tarragon?
Poultry seasoning? A-1?
Thank you, waitress, but I'll wait
For monosodium glutamate.

Bruce Berger

WINE COOLERS

No cork to eye, no sniff, no sip,
No inner fear that you might slip;
No vintage year, no strained pretense,
No sneering sommelier to fence;
No pre-drink ritual or puzzle—
Just open, pour and start to guzzle!

Bern Sharfman

UPWARDLY MOBILE BEAN CURD

The Calico Fish
gets three bucks a dish
for tutti-fruitti Tofutti.
I think that's snutti.

Bonnie Jacobson

AS I WAS DINING AT THE STEAK HOUSE, MY SIRLOIN SAID TO ME

"Take it from a consort of queens, this idolatry
Of beefy brute flesh, castrated and underbroiled,
Is nothing but your little hymn to power; *your* power;
      your
Trembling adoration before your own medium rare

(O tender tauromachian!) with bread and wine and
      Chanel Number Five—
Libations you pour to potency and the ring's black mass
(Pigsticker at the gates of ivory and horn!);
All those niggling inquisitions you open in the vein . . .

What hostages are you barbecueing now?
With what administrative instruments of the public thing
Are you playing cops and robbers, sun and shadow now
In my old masks? *Belle brute, va!* Go build your bloody
      machine

And stick it up a church; my ghost has a date with a
      queen
Tonight, wilder than Pasiphaë, milk-white as the moon."

Scott Bates

LOVE PORTIONS

"Of all heavy bodies, the heaviest is the woman we have ceased to love."

—Lemontey

He left. Our love was on the rocks,
And I took to the chocolate box.
Depressed and utterly despondent
I fortified myself with fondant.
There's never been another man . . .
A bite or two of marzipan.
When passion play became passé,
Sweet solace was marrons glacé.
And keeping me from misery:
A little French patisserie.
I'm haunted by a wistful tune,
I think it's called "Eclair de lune."
Bereft, I wander in a fog
Of strudel mit a bit of schlag.
When love descended to a plateau
I never swallowed pride—just gâteau.
He drove me to hi-cal dejection,
The object of all my confection.
And now love's gone, I'm overcome
With heavy heart and heavy bum.
If only he'd come back to stay
I could exist on Perrier.

Another love? I'll never risk it. . . .
Well, maybe after one more biscuit.

Joan Van Poznak

LIVING ALONE

It's amazing
how many more things
you do naked than before.
Today I made waffles.

D. Scott Taylor

THE BEETS POEM

Beets: now there's a subject.
Dark red, rounded, hard as—
well, hard as beets.

I know a woman
who grew a garden last summer,
planted it with nothing
but lettuce and beets.
The lettuce didn't grow
but she had plenty of slugs
and beets, plenty of beets.
Now whenever anyone visits her
she takes them down cellar,
says, "See my beets?"
And there they are, pickled,
row after row of dark red jars
no one will ever open.

Someone else I know
always asks for beets, no matter
what kind of restaurant we're in.
Even at the beach
he'll go up to the hot dog stand.

"Got any beets?" he'll say.
And when the man at the grill
just stares at him, he sighs
and turns away, and spends
half an hour just gazing at the waves.

I know what you're thinking.
Why don't I introduce these friends,
have them both to dinner
one night, serve vegetarian?
It's not so easy.
Remember, beets is our subject,
and beets is what I hate about them both.

Katharyn Machan Aal

A SOCIAL ENGAGEMENT

Perhaps they will read you an amusing letter—
a hoax appointing your hostess
a meat inspector.

Someone's niece may be there—
who has heard of your work
and imagined a meeting.

You may sit by a broker who set off once from Chad
to look for gorillas.
Oh, he'd have stories to tell.

Well, Charles and Gladys will be there anyway,
and the drinks will be good,
and nothing much will be expected of you.

Knute Skinner

FAUX PAS

Waiting seems to be best. Your remark might
balance on edge—maybe no one will notice
when it falls. After a pause, all at the table
shift their attention. You brush crumbs into your hand.

Maybe you will be forgotten. Maybe a tornado
will scatter this day and you will crawl from the wreckage,
knock off the survivors, and emigrate. Years
will pass. Vines will tangle all over this hemisphere.

In the jungle where you live wild animals will snarl at
       night,
and you will love that sound, so definite: "Ok, so I said
       it."

William Stafford

AFTER DINNER

At table they talk interminably.
They talk of Anne, they talk of Pat,
They talk of you, they talk of me,
They talk of this and they talk of that.

They talk shop, they talk clothes, they talk cash, they talk
       cars,
They talk big, they talk back, they talk up, they talk down.
They talk of themselves for hours and hours,
And they talk about *us* on the way back to town.

David Cram

A REPLY

to answer
yr letter
which never
came,

I hate
you
too.

Jay Dougherty

KNITTING-SITTING SONG

The knots
some knitters knit
are not
as tight as knots
knotted
by other knitters.

The ways
some sitters sit
are not
as beautiful
as the sitting
sat
by some other sitters.

James Steel Smith

XERXES AND XANTHIPPE

I axe you sir this paradox,
the proxy of an oxymoron:
Sol's ox his "burning Axel doth allay"
and "all the way to Biloxi" at that.
Clorox and Ajax on a Xerox
of this would make a palimpsest.

Inexorably "exemplars of art," athletes
such as the Red (absit solar plexus Yaz)
or their peers the Paw Sox or foxy
White ones with reflexes; such
as "roommates with shortest
last names: Roe and Coe"; pax

and whoa, a hoax jinxed by a subplot
of a heterodox relaxed prexy
with ox-eyed coxswain
broken out in complex pox
(he et lox perhaps? exuding toxins).
Explicit mit chiasmus:
biceps around execrable lax doxy
(non et ux) exeunt duo in taxi.

Caroline Knox

COCKS AND CROWS

Everybody knows
that it's the Cock that crows.
If it were cleverer or more knowing
the *Crow* would do the crowing!

Gavin Ewart

GARZA

garza, n.f. Gauze; lint; (Zool.) heron; jaw of a horse.
—*Cassell's Italian Dictionary*

Garza is a funny word
since it can mean a kind of bird

but also lint, and also gauze,
and also, in the plural, jaws

of horses; so, were one to say,
"I'm sad. My *garza* is away,"

that could mean, "Someone took my bone."
"My heron left me all alone."

"My gauze has slipped." "I've lost my lint."
The listener would need some hint

and still might not be very sure
of just what to console you for.

A word like *garza* makes one wish
for simple words like "peach" or "dish"

where even when the meaning's double
at least you know why you're in trouble.

Bruce Bennett

GUTES AND EULAS

When Gutenberg met Eula Snopes
She raised in him unprintable hopes.
But very soon he ran aground
Upon her earthiness profound.
   "You're not for me, although you're ripe,"
   Said G.: "I like the movable type."

When Scheherezade met Billy the Kid,
The sands gained heat from what they did.
He gave her stolen golden watches.
She gave his gun six buenas notches—
   Then stayed up nights one thousand one
   Novelizing what they'd done.

When Don Juan met Sue Barton, Nurse,
He said, "I guess one could do worse,"
Half-heartedly. Of sterner stuff
Our Sue was made. She said, "Oh fluff!
   You are a complex. Even an ism.
   Can you back it up with gism?"

When Mickey Spillane met Guinevere,
He stated, "Me, I don't know fear.
My fists are deadly, so's my rod.
And I know how to treat a brod."
   "Oh yes, I know: Ladies and Lords.
   I've had it all before, with swords."

When Gypsy Rose Lee met Jack the Ripper,
"Well," he said, "so you're a stripper."
"Sure am, Honey." Then he said,

"Wouldn't you rather be an angel instead?"
  "No, I wouldn't; I'm an artiste."
  "Well I am a surgeon and . . . sort of a priest."

When Becky Sharp met Dr. Johnson
(When both were speaking at U. of Wisconsin),
He grumbled, "Tell me why you shook
Off my lexicographical book."
  "I'm a young lady of action, not diction."
  "Noble words—Miss Popular Fiction."

When Mary Poppins met Genghis Khan,
She told him, "Put your rain-boots on."
"My *rain-boots!*" thundered Genghis—"What!?"
"Say a little jingle and then it's not
  Hard to remember: 'Oh, it's puddly. . . .' "
  "Kill her. Bring me something cuddly."

When Job met *la belle dame sans merci*
He said, "So what can you do to me?
For I've been dumped on by Jehovah."
"Yes, but when *I* mess you over,
  I can make your testes shrink
  Just by choosing not to wink."

When Lee Harvey Oswald met Lady MacBeth,
She said, "Do you boggle, Lee Harvey, at death?"
"I don't guess so, I've been to Russia."
"Now here's a man! I won't have to pussia?"
  "Nah. Not me." "Oh great brave foil!"
  "You CIA, Castro, or rich Texas oil?"

When *la belle dame sans merci* met Sade,
The first words out of her mouth were, "*God.
You* think you're tough with all those tricks?"
"Eh," he shrugged. Their respective quicks
    Appeared uncut. Then, "You p.o.'d?"
    He blurted out. "You *wish*," she crowed.

When Frank Sinatra met Molly Bloom,
He sang mellow, filled the room.
Yes she said Yes. He sang smooth and low.
Yes she said Yes. He sang My Way. No
    She said: Sure I'm willing to go along
    But that she said is a terrible song.

When Friedrich Nietszche met Lois Lane,
He found there were notions she'd not entertain:
His. "I know Clark Kent as well as Su-
Perman," she said. "Guess which one you
    Remind me of." He glared and then
    Went out and addressed a group of men.

Roy Blount Jr.

THE BOY & THE WOLF

the boy cried wolf
and the shepherds came
and the wolf did not come

the boy cried wolf
and the wolf came
and the shepherds did not come

aesop! cried the boy
aesop! cried the wolf
and aesop came

Reed Whittemore

A SHORT EPIC POEM IN THE ENGLISH LANGUAGE SUMMARIZING THE ILIAD, THE ODYSSEY, AND THE AENEID

The Greeks invaded Troy, they sacked and sailed home.
Aeneas wandered off, his children founded Rome.

James S. Koch

MY RUMI-NATION*

Roughly stated
in Sufi terms:
the secret of bird flight
rests in the worms.

Julia Older

* Sufi poet *Jalāl al-Dīn Rūmī* (1207-73) expressed mystical thought through symbols.

FOOD PROCESSOR

(after Edna St. Vincent Millay)

The gadget works at top speed—
It really can't be faulted.
It slices, grinds, purees and kneads—
But all I make is malteds.

L. L. Zeiger

ON FIRST LOOKING INTO CHAPMAN'S REFRIGERATOR

Whatever it was
It's covered with fuzz.

Edmund Conti

A FRENCH WRITER NAMED SARTRE

There was a French writer named Sartre
Who got off to a pretty good startre.
But as year followed year,
It got painfully clear
He was longer on wind than on artre.

Weldon Kees

THE VAUNTING SONG OF LOUIS L'AMOUR

Zane is in heaven
    And I in the saddle
Alone carry on the
    Saga of twaddle.

So, readers in force,
    Come join the remuda.
I'll show you a dude who
    Can milk a dead horse.

Come ride with me
    And you will be thrilled
How often a cliché
    Gets up to be killed.

Ernest Kroll

WAITING FOR THE DETECTIVE

The detective is late. He called us here,
to this expensive living room to tell
which of us is a killer. One is. Me?
Ha. I came to use the crystal. The bell

one by one announces who has come. I
drink: the lush. Was I too drunk
that night to cut the throat? My alibi,
my excuse for everything, is—I was.

The gambler had lost at black jack. Power
brokers witnessed it. They'll come forward if—
and only if—required. That same hour
the divorcée was coupling with the cad.

The older sister, tortured by her heart,
was sedated in a single room (damn!),
and her physician/connoisseur of art,
a secret addict, saw her there. Kismet.

One or two I do not know. Cops? Could be.
(Or not. One giggled in the other's ear.)
Everyone. My finger on the rim—high "C"—
makes the detective's friend frown. Where is he?
Lost? Hurt? Maybe worse. They begin to stand.
I pour my sixth. Or seventh. You know me.

Michael Cadnum

FOOD DIRECTOR'S TESTIMONY

Often she wears bon bon colors,
a lemon sweater, a coconut cape.

On the day she appeared
wearing lime slacks

lime sherbert was served for dessert
in the dining hall. That very night

she was found slumped on her bed:
I was there. I swear she was

wearing a peach-flan peignoir,
her hair done up in meringue.

Nancy Simpson

KING ALFRED EXPLAINS IT

(A Poem for Students of Intellectual History)

The conqueror of Rome behaved
better than the Romans had expected.
They found their walls and women saved,
their rights respected,

as likewise proper form: the new
Imperator taxed, not stole, his money,
wore purple, and even listened to
the Senate politely.

A minimum of looting, and
his Ostrogoths had settled down

on what was formerly desert land,
to guard the town

against all other kinds of Goths.
The world was at its rosiest
since men first shed unchristian myths—
go ask Orosius.

Boethius demurred. Not that
Theordoric was a barbarian
(educated in Istanbul!), but
he was an Arian,

a heretic: in mind all ill,
though not in deed; the Devil's proxy!
Boethius would trade good will
for orthodoxy.

He coveted Theodoric's head,
was found out and condemned for it;
he thought that God must guard the Good,
and found the opposite.

He was thrown into jail, deprived
of all his goods save ink and quill;
wrote he'd be hanged who had been wived,
but by free will.

His sentence was predestinate,
yet not predestinate, he reckoned,
since all eternity's innate
in half a second.

Thus he consoled himself for odium
and loss of honors and palaces

(himself and the next millennium)
with pious fallacies,

and mentioned that there were no such worries
in the first bright golden age of the world,
when everyone ate nuts and berries,
and no one quarrelled.

G. N. Gabbard

COUP DE GRACE

If Lady Godiva had cut off
The tresses she loosed
She might have got taxes abolished
Instead of reduced.

Mildred Luton

QUEEN ANNE'S LEGS

Queen Anne had bowlegs
which ended in small,
graceful club feet.

She was all curves.
The king loved
to sit in her lap.

Jane Flanders

PISA VISA

Physicists believe that they have discovered a previously unknown antigravity force that challenges Galileo's theory. They call it "the hypercharge force."

News Item.

We've all learned about that geezer
Standing on the Tower of Pisa
    Dropping cannon balls
And were taught that he was great at
Predetermining the rate at
    Which an object falls.

But, Galileo Galilei,
Now your feet are turning clayey!
    Long were you enshrined,
But they've dealt a frightful K.O.
That has left you, Galileo,
    Gravely undermined.

Science, grown so highfalutin,
Also is refutin' Newton,
    Giving him the prod,
Gouging out a cavity
In his law of gravity—
    Where 'twill end, knows God!

Science can be unremitting,
'Stead of tending to its knitting
    Like Madame DeFarge,
Rushing into print to tell
What all shoppers know too well:
    The force of hyper-charge.

Felicia Lamport

I WISH I WERE LIVING IN YOUR CENTURY

Victoria—choosing, willy nilly
among the arts or the artillery,
society's pillars or its pillory.
Oh, to have frittered one's heart away
watching fritillaries flutter and stray
past punting dons and demi-mondes
on sleepy streams and Sunday ponds!

A. L. Lazarus

THE QUEEN TAKES DRAWING LESSONS
FROM EDWARD LEAR

The Queen of England drew but one
    Self-portrait. Said Her Majesty,
"The masterpiece, my Lords, is done.
    Now tell me what you see."
Her Lords began to weep because
Each knew exactly what it was
    But none could quite agree.

The first one cried, "Beef Stroganoff?"
    The second said, "Hyena?"
The third exclaimed, "It's slightly off . . .
    The Coast of Argentina!"
They more they wept, the more they guessed—
    "Potatoes in their skin?"
"A Tuning Fork!" "A Buzzard's Nest!"
    "The Duke of Wellington?"

"You nincompoops!" the royal jaw
  Shot back, and cracked the chandelier.
"I'll have you know I learned to draw
  From Master Mr. Lear.
Go fetch the famous lad for me!"
Her Lords looked up. "Your Majesty,
  He's standing in the rear."

As Lear approached the Head of State,
  He saw that quirk of art
And thought of . . . Beef upon a Plate?!
  It nearly broke his heart.
But all he said was "Ah, my Queen?!"
  And fell into her lap
As large and lean as the Argentine.
  She smiled. "You clevah chap!"

J. Patrick Lewis

EDWARD LEAR FINDS PARADISE
(AND LOSES IT)

Mr. Lear had widely traveled
But the roads he took were graveled
   And his pheet were getting sore.
So he thought it wise to settle
Where a Pobble wouldn't pedal—
Where the Jumblies like to meddle—
   In the Hills of Chankly Bore.

Then a sudden Rural Raven
Phlew him to that happy haven
   On the phar Italian shore.
It was there he made a bee-line—
With his phat and phavorite pheline—
And they both enjoyed the sea-line
   So, they thought, for evermore.

Oh the days they passed as princes
Eating chocolate shrimps and quinces,
   Drinking periwinkle wine.
Though he suffered phits and phainted,
Mr. Lear was well-acquainted
With the landscapes that he painted
   And the cat was doing phine.

But a lady took a notion
To erect between the otion
   And his haven a hotel.
If he could he would have phought her
For the sun and pea-green water,
But he said, "Oh pitter-potter!"
   And he bade a sad pharewell.

J. Patrick Lewis

OLD FOSS (THE CAT) RECALLS HIS LIFE WITH MR. LEAR

You'd say when we ate a late breakfast
    Of jelly or jam in a jar,
"A sliver of ham is upon your pajamas.
    How perfectly messy you are!"

I'd bury my head in your pillow,
    Falling flat in the fold of the fluff.
You'd curse at the blanket and suddenly yank it
    Away, but I knew it was bluff.

And the mice I would catch in the garden—
    Or trap in the trunk of a tree—
I wish had been fatter. "Oh, what does that matter,"
    You said, "won't you share them with me?"

Once the postman delivered a letter
    With a ding and a dong on the door.
You replied to that twaddle by vinegar bottle
    And pushed it away from the shore.

After forty-four thousand adventures
    Afoot and afloat and afar,
"One more trip in a tub'll be buckets of trouble,"
    You said. "Let us stay where we are."

And we did. And I say with a sniffle—
    Oh piffle and puffle and posh!—
Although you are minus the title "Your Highness,"
    I bow to the King of High Bosh.

                                    J. Patrick Lewis

CLERIHEWS

St. Jerome
abandoned brush and comb
and bread and jam and everything nice.
He did it on divine advice.

*

Robert Herrick
wasn't your run of the mill cleric.
When served a smooth white breakfast egg
he thought of Julia's leg.

*

George the Fourth
wore kilts to visit the North.
What an appalling yardage
encircled His Royal Lardage!

Vonna Adrian

Hernando DeSoto
Never took a good photo,
But he was quite a charmer
When he took off his armor.

Margaret Blaker

Walter Savage Landor
walked out on the verander,
and there Macauley
met him with a verbal volley.

*

Poor George Gissing
was found missing—
but I don't think that's a sound
use of "found."

*

Sir Walter Raleigh
loved to shout, "By Golly!"—
which James the First dreaded—
so James had him beheaded.

James Steel Smith

"When Wyndham Lewis
  drew us,"
  said Edith Sitwell,
"we satwell."

Bonnie Jacobson

Scott Joplin
wore suits made of poplin
or from bean bags—
but he tore them to rags.

Gavin Ewart

Shirley Temple
Made the most of each dimple.
Blonde she isn't now, a pity,
For she used to be so pretty.

*

You could count on Mae West
To keep you abreast and abreast
Of things. Than she no one was fonder
Of a classy *double-entendre.*

Paul Curry Steele

Margaret Sanger,
when the boys used to bang her,
must have felt a little cold—
knowing her own birth had not been controlled.

*

Gloria Steinem—
would she wine 'em and dine 'em
if she wore the pants?
Fat chance.

Tom Riley

E. C. Bentley
Knew, evidently,
That those who can eat just one potato crisp or write just
    one clerihew
Are very few.

David Jacobs

CLERIHEW COUPLES

Elizabeth Barrett
Whispered over her claret,
"My father's a slob;
Get me out of here, Bob."

Robert Browning
Thought she was clowning
Till she rose in a rush
And handed him Flush.

*

D. H. Lawrence
Viewed with abhorrence
The lay of the land—
That's why he was banned.

Along came Frieda,
Who said, "Bert, you need a
Place where they don't act so prissily.
Let's try Sicily."

*

Alice B. Toklas
Said, "We'd go broke less
If you wrote something simple, sweet,
Like the Lady from Wimpole Street.

Gertrude Stein
Thought that was fine,
And began to compose
"A rose is a rose. . . ."

*

Thomas Hardy
Didn't like to party.
But that posed no dilemma
Since neither did Emma.

Roberta Simone

SONS OF THE RIGHT HAND

Like Jonson's son, I am of the right hand.
And Jonson père, he had the same first name.
The intellect of Franklin was so grand,
He gained in many fields a lasting fame.

Disraeli led the English Parliament,
Wrote novels and was later made an Earl.
Harrison was his nation's President,
And Hogan set the golfing world awhirl.

Millions of parents heeded Doctor Spock
While Shahn's art leaned to themes political.
The "King of Swing" and London's tower clock
Both bear this name, ancient and Biblical.

Despite all this I find, with some chagrin,
Few children nowadays named Benjamin.

Benjamin Hochman

THE CONSOLATIONS OF ETYMOLOGY, WITH FANFARE

Zany—from *Giovanni* (John)
    (Through Venetian *Zanni*).
Denim—from *de Nîmes*. Right on,
    Sing hey nonny nonny!
Once I thought my name—well, blah.
Zany in denim, though! Ta-DAH!

John Frederick Nims

AN AGED RECTOR NAMED FIDDLE

An aged rector named Fiddle
Refused an honorary degree.
Said he, "Bad enough being Fiddle,
Without being Fiddle D.D."

Robert Phillips

HAVE YOU? I HAVE NEVER!

Have you ever met a pundit?
I mean, off the printed page?
Do they have a sense of humor?
Are they kind as well as sage?
Though the papers quote 'em daily
(For their knowledge is profound),
I have never met a pundit—
Don't they ever get around?

Have you ever met a maven?
That is, far from center stage?
Are their insights truly brilliant?
Do they earn a fancy wage?
Though their expertise is legend
(For their judgments carry weight),
I have never met a maven—
Don't they ever circulate?

If you're ever with a pundit
And a maven near Antietam,
Please don't hesitate to call me—
I would dearly love to meet 'em!

Ned Pastor

NEAR-MISS EDDY

Doris Humphrey's father
owned Euclid Beach where we
went on the rollycoaster & the dodgem &
Hart Crane's folks who lived in Chagrin Falls
owned Crane's Canary Cottage at 105th &
Euclid where we went for
ice cream sodas sundaes & Tin Roofs when
we didn't go to Hoffman's after
Saturday morning drawing class &
Sherwood Anderson worked for my second
best friend's rich uncle who manufactured
wheeled goods in Elyria & Jack London was
an uncle or a cousin or something of my
best friend who was older and had my
dead mother's name insideout &
Phoebe and Alice Carey poets in
case you didn't have them in school
were Grandma's cousins & in
our first teens my second best friend's
rich aunt and uncle took her out
west to call on her aunt's friend who
was Douglas Fairbanks' exwife and
Douglas Fairbanks Jr came in just enough
older to be an insufferable adolescent
(simply wonderful men are usually
impossible adolescents) & on the train
tripped over Ramon Novarro's cane the
handsomest man in films but
short but who knew and when my
little boy who looked like an angel was
two & we took the train for Newton Center
to visit friends and sat in the very first
seat in the car all to ourselves in the

very last seat in the car facing me when
we had to go that way looking right at
me but not seeing me was Rudy Vallee
whom i didn't gave a fig for but
in our latter days when he cracked
up singing There is a Tavern in the Town i
did too & think he's wonderful &

you may touch me
but it won't get you anything

Elizabeth Eddy

LITTLE ELEGY

for Johnny Olson, d. October 1985

O Johnny O,
your game-show

tones still live,
your merry imperative

in its karma of reruns
quickens

our night,
the price finally right,

the big prize won:
come on down!

Michael McFee

ELEGY FOR MR. ED, THE TALKING HORSE

"a horse is a horse. . . ."

Ed, Ed,
why is everything so real these days?
You were the last talking horse
the world will ever see.
Now they have machines that talk
and become heroes.

Reading of your death,
I think of poor Wilbur
left to fend without you
against his wife Kay and neighbor Herb,
telling them, "He talked, he really. . . ."

I wipe the tears from my eyes
and scratch my dog's ears,
tell him you have died.
I get down on all fours
and look into his eyes.
I say, "Speak, speak,"
and he barks, barks.

Jim Daniels

ARMED CONFLICT

At concerts and such
   Where the public meets,
Whose elbows have rights
   To the arms of the seats?

Pier Munn

SILENT LOVER

He was soft on Swanson,
   For Mae Busch he had a crush,
He'd tickle Pola and extol her
   But she gave him that Nazi bum's rush.

His heart swelled up for Bara,
   For Clara he carried a torch,
He pined for Banky to drop her hankie—
   La Rocque pushed him right off the porch.

And all that time he was silent
   And getting increasingly balky.
Then darling Marlene allowed him to gain her—
   Thank god, he came in with the talkie!

Edward Watkins

EVERYBODY IN AMERICA IS AT THE MOVIES

My windows open onto Wall Street
Where ropes of money
Are tying me into knots. Ho hum:
Another Gregory Peck morning,
Neither too hot nor too cold,
With Mae as Medusa
Making the Hudson rock.
Everybody in America is at the movies.
A screenplay writer calls from L.A.:
"What I want to do,
Nobody will pay me for, &
What they pay me for,
I do not want to do."
So what else is new? Ho hum.
The sun, with its friendly persuasion,
Is scaling my city's fair banks,
The Gary Cooper rocks.
My parents are flying down
From Marx Brothers' Metropolis,
Taking a slight detour
Over the Paramount Mountains.
LANA TURNER HAS COLLAPSED,
But that's in another poem.
If it happens to movie stars,
Then it really happens.
My own life, for example,
Is further down the line,
Further than I can possibly imagine.
Tomorrow some Bette Davis rain,
Crippling,
Coupled with Humphrey Bogart fog.

All the airports will be closed.
Frankly, my dear,
I tell my friend from L.A.,
I don't give a damn.

Louis Phillips

DUKE

It took him years to get out of the mailroom
at Whitehead Metals but he did it,
made 70 bucks a week in posting,
and though he finally got his figures neat
he always had trouble remembering which was sheet and
which was slab, and confused the ID's of pipe with OD's,
and sometimes stared at the numbers on the PO's
in his ham fists for minutes before
he subtracted the poundage from the cards.

One day when the boss was out Jackie Olson yelled
"Hey—Duke took the Mrs. to a movie last night,
The Ten Commandments. How'd you like it Duke?
D'ja understand what it was about?"
And we waited while Duke turned his huge head
like a buffalo with its horns down and said
"yeah, I liked it, it was about
the beginnin of the Catlic religion,
up yours."

Ed Ochester

THE PRIMITIVE ASTRONOMER

"There is an exploratory, open-road outward-bound
spirit that has marked us since our hunter-gatherer
days."

—Carl Sagan

The boundaries of dull straight thinking blur
as they could never blur for a mere dunce.
Professor Sagan seems to think that once
he was a hunter and a gatherer.

Those narrow shoulders pitted themselves against
the grubby power of a resistant root.
That brow, so celebrated and astute,
was furrowed, and that Sagan belly tensed,

to meet with levelled spear the charges of
the cave bear and the sabertooth. That voice
discussed, urbanely, arrowheads of choice.
Those loins sought humdrum reproductive love.

The picture clears, and now we understand:
the primate still employs his grasping hand.

Tom Riley

BIG BANG

When I saw the squirrel
going down the branch
to where the bird feeder
hangs, I stepped out
on the porch and slammed
the screen door, once.
Then I went back inside
and sat down. The gods
have an easy time of it.

Jay Meek

AT THE BRIEFING FOR CREATION DAY

"And now," said God,
(assuming there were Forms
—and some still do—)
"are there any questions?"
Said a bird to God:
"*Bones* in my wings?
Man, are you mad?
I gotta fly.
Gimme the stuff like
feathers and things
like I mean crazy with
fluff for the high."
Said God to that bird:
"*Bones* in your wings.
And in a particular order."

Mary Jean Irion

GEEK

He walks. He talks. He sits to eat.
He watches, full of furtive mirth,
A well-attended bitch in heat.
He spits upon the patient earth.

He frowns. He wipes his beery mouth
And squints to give the sky a glance.
He poses, gazing toward the south.
He shrugs. He hitches up his pants.

He whistles "Jake the Mountaineer"
And taps his finger on his knee.
He scratches just behind his ear.
He throws a pebble at a tree.

So this is Man! He's odd, it's true—
And, if you really want to know,
A trifle dull. Yes, *entre nous*,
The porpoise makes a better show.

David H. Green

HELENDALE

*Beeeeeeeeeeeeeeeeeeeeeeeeeeeeeeeeeeeeeeeeeeeeeeeeeeeeeeee-
eeeeeeeeeee*

A night wreck out on the highway
left one driver crushed unconscious against the horn,

so: an alfalfa farmer got up
and set fire to his barn, as a beacon, for angels.

He'd been listening, as he lay there, for Gabriel,
and thought that horn was his trumpet blowing the
        Second Coming

all the rest of that night.
Toward morning the barn went out.

Crews came and carried off the wrecked cars,
the hurt and the done for; at sunup

there was only the black smudge of rubber
on the red pavement, charred beams of the barn,

the hulk of a tractor he'd left parked
inside. Red eyed with spent feelings, that farmer,

being up already, went on about his business,
worked on a fence and let in the irrigation

still listening just the same. And his one mistake—
or I'd have to say his other mistake—

was he told the insurance agent how it happened,
was laughed at, got angry, had to quit

the Kiwanis Club after a fight, and he felt lonely
until he thought:

"Well: I reckon if Noah could take it, so can I."

Dick Barnes

JUST GOD

On lines from Emily Dickinson's letters

Who writes these funny accidents
    where railroads meet each other
quite unexpectedly, and gentlemen
    in factories get their heads cut off
    quite informally? The Author

    relates them in such a sprightly
        way, they are quite attractive.
If prayers had any answers to them,
    I should not know the question, for I
    seek and I don't find and knock and

    it is not opened. I wonder
        if God is just—presume that
He is, and 'twas only a blunder of
    Matthew's. Heaven is large, isn't it?
    Then when one is done, is there not

    another, and—and—then if God
    is willing, we are neighbors then.

Lewis Turco

THE CONSCIENCE

The conscience is a built-in feature
That haunts the sinner, helps the preacher.
Some sins it makes us turn and run from,
But most it simply takes the fun from.

Richard Armour

GRACE

The day the Messiah
came to dinner,
she set out the new china.

When she asked Him to say grace,
he only smiled
pointing to His mouthful
of mashed potatoes.

Al Ortolani

RELIGION POEM

The testimony of Muffkin Puffkin unto the
Hebrides. The testimony of *what*? among potsherds,
emblements for the flan and teletherm of the afflicted
provident instanter. The stars hang out
chez Marcus et Galba, "throned and teaching."

Drink this in remembrance of yourself
in case you forget who you are
and Jesus will remind you; bless
your heart of hearts, both sacred and otherwise,
keeping your hands to yourself. And Christo
will wrap you, *awfullae memoriae*, in kneesocks,
turtlenecks, facemasks and earmuffs, with
plenty of Auchinclosses and Katzenbachs,
Leffingwells and Tillinghasts, to speak generally.

Caroline Knox

WORSHIPER

Tithing
every Sunday,
he scrupulously went
to tip his Help the standard ten
per cent.

Gloria A. Maxson

TENDING A COOKOUT IN POURING RAIN
WHILE POPE JOHN PAUL II ARRIVES IN BOSTON

It rains on my bratwurst,
On the roofs of the town
What it rains on the Pope.
Buns become wet white glop.

While the pious absorb
From flasks spiked lemonade,
Along Commonwealth Ave
Glides his waxed motorcade.

Now the smoke of soaked coal
Rises meek as incense.
Leaning heads of cloud scowl
Down with indifference.

O Lord, why hast thou sent
So much sky excrement?
Dost thou cast down a message
On my cold Polish sausage?

Will his ringy hand wave,
Drive aside this cloudburst,
Backward-summoning, save
Abortees? The divorced?

In a muscular creed
Trichinosis may lie.
Go home, Bishop of Rome.
Let these weiners stay dry

That still writhe as in pain
Like shucked souls of the curst.
Father, grant us a rain
Brief as John Paul the First!

X. J. Kennedy

LOOSESTRIFE

It is clear to the clergy
God favors the loosestrife.
Cattails, smartweed, rushes and sedges
concede to that flower: Cayuga,
the Hudson, St. Lawrence and rivers
that fish in the states of New Jersey,
Rhode Island, Vermont and New York.
Not mowing or burning or pulling
or planting competitive stands
of Japanese millet will kill it.

Aggressive and wanton as moonlight
the loosestrife is fecund on other
than wetlands, even abides

on the banks of the eye.
Three minutes of tears
and the weeper cries loosestrife.
Under the moist arms of lovers
tendrils extend.

We hear there are loosestrife riots in Cyprus.
International loosestrife laws will be urged
while The First Botanical Church of the Loosestrife
gathers members to pray for our planet.

Elaine Magarrell

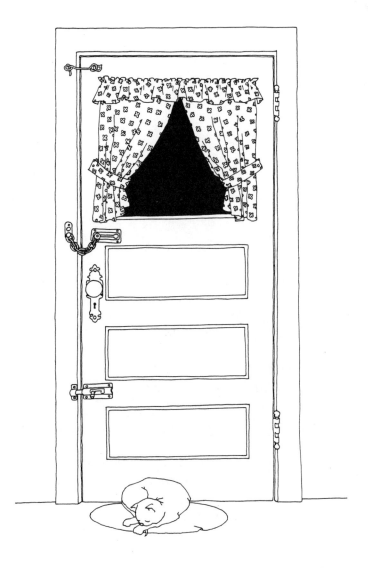

DOMESTIC CRISIS

"Mother! Father! Hurry, hurry!
Something mammoth, fat and furry
Just jumped out of a banana!
It's making off with Adrianna!"

"Hmmm," says Mother, "is it handsome?
Did it not demand a ransom?"
Father frowns. "I must insist
We cross fruit off our shopping list."

X. J. Kennedy

W. D., DON'T FEAR THAT ANIMAL

—after the painting by DeLoss McGraw

My hat leaps up when I behold
    A rhino in the sky;
When crocodiles upon the wing
Perch on my windowsill to sing
All my loose ends turn blue and cold;
    I don't know why.

My knuckles whiten should I hark
    Some lonely python's cry;
Should a migrating wedge of moose
Honk, it can shake my molars loose—
Or when, at heaven's gate, the shark
    Doth pine and sigh.

My socks may slide off at the sight
    Of giant squids on high
Or baby scorpions bubbling up
Inside my morning coffee cup—
Somehow, it spoils my appetite;
    My throat gets dry.

At dawn, I lift my gaze in air
    Cock Robin to espy
And mark instead some bright-eyed grizzly;
The hairs back of my neck turn bristly.
That's foolish since it's clear that they're
    More scared than I.

Such innocent creatures mean no harm;
    They wouldn't hurt a fly.
Still, when I find myself between a
Playful assembly of hyena,

I can't help feeling some alarm;
I've got to try.

W. D. Snodgrass

CREDO

for Antonia Quintana Pigno

This is the song
Cock Robin sung.

This is the breath, forthright and strong,
That carried along the airborne song
Cock Robin sung.

This is the lung, the throat, the tongue,
That fashioned the breath, forthright and strong
To carry along the airborne song
Cock Robin sung.

These are the breezes, east and west,
That swelled the lung, the throat, the tongue,
That shaped the breath, forthright and strong
To carry along the airborne song
Cock Robin sung.

This is the 8-storey-high birds' nest
Blown by the breezes, east and west,
To open the lung, the throat, the tongue
That formed the breath, forthright and strong

To carry along the airborne song
Cock Robin sung.

This is the worm, a creeping pest,
That climbed up the 8-storey-tall birds' nest
Battered by breezes to east and west
That filled out the lung, the throat, the tongue
To drive the breath, forthright and strong,
And carry along the airborne song
Cock Robin sung.

This is the rumor, slimy and sly,
That crept like worms or a crawling pest
To worry the 8-storey roost or nest
Swung by the breezes to east and west
And forcing the lung, the throat, the tongue
To channel the breath, forthright and strong
And carry along the airborne song
Cock Robin sung.

Here's old Mr. Evil who told the lie
That fathered the rumor, smirking and sly,
That bristled like worms or a creepy pest
That gnawed at the 8-storey perch or nest
That lurched as the breeze blew, east and west,
Impelling the lung, the throat, the tongue
That managed the breath, forthright and strong
To carry along the airborne song
Cock Robin sung.

These are dark angels that fly forth and spy
Where old Mr. Evil's telling his lie
That started the rumor, slippery and sly,
To spread like worms, some plague or pest,

Attacking the 8-storey tower or nest
That tilt in the breezes, east and west,
Inflating the lung, the throat, the tongue
To strengthen the breath, forthright and strong
And carry along the airborne song
Cock Robin sung.

Here are pink putti that dogfight the sky
Against the dark angels that fly out and spy,
Then pecked Mr. Evil for telling that lie,
Then checked the vile rumor, insidious and sly,
And fed on the worms, that plump, white pest
Surrounding the 8-storey aerie or nest
That leans in the breezes, east and west,
Inspiring the lung, the throat, the tongue
That mastered the breath, forthright and strong.
To bear along the airiest song
Cock Robin sung.

Here is the void, the blank, black eye
That watches pick putti dogfight the sky
To harry dark angels that fly and spy
While old Mr. Evil still tells his lie
And on goes the rumor, sinuous, sly,
Like worms into hiding or some unknown pest
That lurks near the 8-storey towering nest
Rocked by the breezes from east and from west
Empowering the lung, the throat, the tongue
That guided the breath, forthright and strong,
And saved so long from rot and from wrong
The marvelous lifelong, lovesprung song
Cock Robin sung.

W. D. Snodgrass

CORONER'S INQUEST

Who killed Cock Robin?
Don't you blyme me, says the sparrow;
I gone strictly straight-and-narrow,
Reformed, true-blue, a real straight arrow.
I never done that slob in.

Who saw him die?
Not I, certainly, says the fly;
My dear, this polyhedral eye
Can only make things out nearby.
I mind my own bee's wax; that's my
Alibi.

Who'll wash the body?
We know too well, says the raccoon,
He sang low songs, played the buffoon
In many a roadhouse or saloon
From bawdy midnight to high noon.
It's only fitting that so soon
He's left lowdown and cruddy.

Who'll weave his shroud?
Our local folkarts, says the spider,
Are unbecoming an outsider
Or untraditional fore-slider
Who's rejected every guide or
Guideline, led by spiritual pride or
Sensual passion through a wider
World than we're allowed.

Who'll dig his grave?
I'm committed, says the mole,
To exploring my own hole

Liberated from control
Of any social, prefixed role;
I keep my deep molehood whole
Seeking my true self and soul.
My blind eye's fixed on this goal;
Go find a cave.

Who'll bear his casket?
Count me out there, says the ant.
I'm too small; I simply can't.
With my legion friends, I grant
We might, yet we're all adamant
That unless he should recant
Each lewd song and surreal chant
With their sly, anarchic slant,
Even if we could we shan't
So don't ask it.

Who'll say the last words?
Of course I'd like to, says the parrot;
I'm aware that all his merit
Was so rare we can't compare it,
Yet my grief and great despair at
This sad loss, if I should share it,
Is so vast, I couldn't bear it.
Then besides, my friends don't care at
All for anyone who'd dare it.
Those that sing strange songs inherit
Faint praise—few and fast words.

All the beasts of earth and air
Fell a-weaselin' and a-bobbin'
When they heard of the death
Of poor Cock Robin.

W. D. Snodgrass

HIS TOYS

We planned to keep your first toys,
preserve them; one day,
when you were grown, lead you
to a secret closet, watch you
pull wide, amazed,
re-discover your treasures.
But we can't; you're eating them.

Michael Dennis Browne

SHARPER THAN A SERPENT'S TOOTH

King Lear's canon of sins, in sooth,
Possesses some degree of truth.
But sure ingratitude is mild.
Wouldst thou prefer a sleepless child?

Paul Sawyer

OLECRANON

Behind the elbow joint,
On the little-finger side,
Lurks a tiny compass point.
If bumped, worlds collide
And empires fall inside,
And poisonous snakes wiggle
All day and into the night—
The numb sensation of a giggle
Falling to its knees to pray.
Amnesiac, clown, and stowaway.

Ernest Slyman

THE MADNESS OF A HEADMISTRESS

Don't be a fool, don't go to school,
don't put a foot outside—
old Miss Oysterley
is eating bubblegum,
Sellotape, tin tacks and Tide!

Be like a mouse, stay in the house—
her mouth is open wide—
weird Miss Oysterley
is drinking printer's ink,
paint and insecticide!

Don't go near the Head, just stay in bed—
jump in a box and hide—
old Miss Oysterley
is fond of the little ones,
roasted or frittered or fried!

It's very sad, she's gone quite mad,
her brain is quite putrefied—
poor Miss Oysterley
munching through Infants I
that once was her joy and her pride!

Gavin Ewart

Note: Sellotape is a transparent adhesive tape. *Infants I* is of course a class in British primary school.

OH, NOW I SEE . . .

When your pre-schooler brings you
A drawing he's made,
To be too exact is the danger:
When you say,
"What a marvelous furry raccoon!"—
And it turns out to be the Lone Ranger.

Keith Casto

SCHOOL CHEER (PROGRESSIVE STYLE)

A-root-toot-toot
A-root-toot-toot
We're from the Goose Egg Institute!
We are not rough
We are not tough
We don't believe in competitive stuff.
We learn ballet
And art through play
And how to be well-liked, each day.
We're taught to weave
And fly a kite
And make a good milk custard.
We cannot read
Or add or write
But, boy, are we adjusted!

Alma Denny

LIGHT AND SHADOW

This knee-high nymph is three-year Johnny
Tear-wet and water-wet and sunny.
He stubbed his toe for the brook is stony.
Just stub your own if you think it's funny.

See how the sun picks out his body
While all around is dark and shady.
He's still in tears and a bit unsteady.
Call it a light-and-shadow study.

You should have heard the dappled mixture:
His wailing and the chuckling water,
Our words of comfort and our laughter.
Just then somebody snapped the picture.

Robert Francis

MY SON, THE TUBA PLAYER

Someone playing, Lord
Oom-pah-pah
Someone playing, Lord
Oom-pah-pah
Someone practicing
Oom-pah-pah
Lord, Lord, oom-pah-pah.

Edmund Conti

TUNING THE TRUMPET

Sally sat
upon her horn
without intent to do it.

Worriedly,
hurriedly
she picked it up and blew it.

She'd mashed
it flat,
but didn't carp

because
before
the horn blew sharp.

Noa Spears

RIDDLE WITH GUESSES

1

See how each of them heaps its own wee pile,
Each in its own niche, each keeping its eyes
Fixed on these intrinsically lovely forms.
From time to time a worm goes by,
Unsettling its repose. *Is it a rose?*

No, guess again.

2

When to their horde the black thieves come
And make away with weighty haul,

Their hall remains, and all it thinks
Is, "I'll restore." *A corpse? A skull?*

No, guess once more.

3

When the day comes that they pass on,
You'll get no undivided pie.
Though not your uncles they are kin
And you have got them in your pants.

Ants.

You guessed it.

Tom Disch

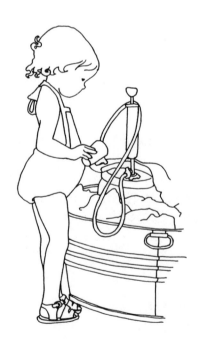

BAILEY

the day he shot the lion
i heard bailey himself come running up
shout for old lavender his elephant gun
and his winkie

These are the words overheard
in last night's dream,
fraught with the keen sense of meaning
you feel in a dream
and spoken aloud by a woman
in articulate tones.
A woman who knows Bailey himself,
whoever he is.

Who Bailey is,
I'm sure I don't know.
He seems to be someone who calls an elephant gun
Old Lavender,
and too, he seems ready to use such a gun
on a lion.

But is he someone as well who won't ahunting go
without his winkie?
Whatever that is.

I'm sure I don't know.

Knute Skinner

ALPHABET SOUP

> "And the Lord God brought them unto
> Adam to see what he would call them:
> and whatsoever Adam called every living
> creature, that was the name thereof."
>
> (Genesis 2:19)

The aardvark and the armadillo
In the beginning had no name;
Nor did the bear and the cat and the dingo
As into the Garden of Eden they came.

Earwigs and ferrets, gerbils and hawkmoths,
None of them knew what the others were called;
None of them knew that some seagulls are herring,
None of them knew that some eagles are bald.

Oh what a grand onomastic confusion!
What grounds for epistemological doubt!
Then up stepped a monkey called homo erectus
Who made up a language and sorted them out.

David Cram

THE MOCKING BIRD AND THE OWL

kalamazoo toledo springfield springfield
kalamazoo toledo great salt lake
    sang a mocking bird way high in an old yew
while a small hoot owl hooted a small hoo
and again hoo
in the same yew
provoking the mocking bird
to walla walla winter park winter park worcester
walla walla winter park great salt lake

to which the owl replied with another small hoo
and again hoo
and all through the dell the duet was heard with
        equanimity
except by a boy psychiatrist from the big city
who sat in his cell at the lone motel in the dell
and was sad that the owl was sad
        for surely the owl *was* sad
that he was not a bird
who could kalamazoo toledo springfield springfield
like the mocking bird?

of course the boy psychiatrist
knew what city boys know about woods and fields
which was that they are an emptiness
waiting for city boys
who know how to conquer an emptiness
                and be a success
in the emptiness
so the city boy spoke to the owl
                and said owl
I'm sure that you have been trying to take your small hoo
and make it into a kind of a kalamazoo
and I'm sure that you dream of doing toledo too
and possibly walla walla
but I think you should know that what you dream you can
        do
is not in the cards for you you are an owl
and owls hoo
a fact that I think you should know so I pass it on
in this practical book of mine
on page nine
in which you will see that the moral
is about pride and all
and how it might have a fall

on an owl
        well the owl
spun his head around twice and all the way back again
and took the boy's book and ruffled it to page nine
and read it
        and then did opine
city boy you are indubitably a smart cookie when not in
        this dell
with an education in one of those institutions of higher
        learning
        of which I have heard tell
but as for page nine
it has nothing at all to do with this case of mine
I am not hooked
        on the mocking bird
I do not blab
        like the mocking bird
and though I could easily
sing kalamazoo toledo springfield springfield
kalamazoo toledo great salt lake
        like the mocking bird
I don't because it's too showy much too showy
        and too absurd
you are on the wrong track
        here is your book back

at which point the mocking bird
sang oconomowoc penobscot tucson tucson
oconomowoc penobscot great salt lake
and the owl said hoo

Reed Whittemore

FABLE OF THE CURIOUS CROW
AND THE DEVIOUS WEEVIL

"Could you tell me the meaning
And nature of Evil?"
Asked a curious crow
Of a wily young weevil

Whom the former had formed
The intention to eat:
"Why, yes," said the weevil,
"All Evil is Meat."

So the crow went to live
With his unmarried daughter
To a tranquil old age
On fried okra and water,

While the weevil went out
To the Drive-in to eat,
Had a steak and French fries
And perished *tout de suite*.

MORAL
Most everyone makes
The most dreadful mistakes,
But a Drive-in's
Misteaks
Are the toughest.

Scott Bates

JOB'S TURKEY: A COMMENTARY

I should be vigilant: the Sodomite
Merchant is expected any day,
And with the sheep dead, who knows
Where his barnyard eyes might rove?
Not on this bird, a peeping Tom
Among the oxen bones, scavenging for mites
With an eye for trouble and an ear for news.

Not that much else could go wrong,
With the old guy sulking, the wife yelling *Curse!*
You should live like this? Get it over.
Which is not bad advice: living in ashes
With open sores and a screaming wife
Is no Eden, especially
For a former gentlemen farmer
As well-heeled as anyone before it happened.
Now, as he tiptoes among the tree stumps
And relieves himself without so much as a pot,
It isn't surprising that he wonders out loud
What miscalculation brought it on,
While those bores who showed up afterwards
Sit scratching and passing wind,
Saying *Admit it. It's all your fault.*

Easy thing for them to say, except
They can't figure it out either:
How old Straight-And-Narrow,
The pillar of the community
Whose worst offense was kicking the hounds,
Could get the holy shaft but insist he's clean.
What can they tell their kids?
Be nice? Don't talk back? Clean your plates?

Suck rocks. But: if he curses,
The worm was there, it was there all the time,
Waiting to be spat between his teeth:
He is cast into a snare by his own feet,
And they can go home.

Yep, he had it coming. You bet.
Eat your asparagus.

A lone camel. Not the Sodomite:
He keeps several for companionship.
Maybe one of the locals bringing tidings.
There's something funny in the wind,
And lately, going to and fro in the earth
My own scratchings have revealed
Signs of curious events, concerning which
I should be vigilant, and with any luck
Bear only witness to.

Carl Judson Launius

$$E = MC^{round}$$

The worm in Newton's apple said:
The Universe is round and red;
It swells to ripen, fall, and rot.
(She knew a lot that Newt knew not.)

Ann Deagon

I-35, SOUTH OF WACO

The Ford pickup, painted red but rusted, straddled
the yellow line. Both back fenders were dented in.

It was almost noon in Waco. The truck stalled in
the sun, in time, in Texas. As if in a dream, it
began to move forward slowly.

There were three of them in the cab. Two men and a
dog. One was brushing his teeth. One was drinking
from a brown bottle. The dog was driving.

William Virgil Davis

THE ERRAND BOY'S DAY OFF

Lying in bed
watching my cat
watching a bee
traversing the window,
looking for an exit, I suppose.
O existential bee!

Hands behind my head,
arms spread like wings,
I am considering getting up.
It will be some time
before I reach a decision.

Kurt Lipschutz

TO THE EXTENT THAT I HAVEN'T A CAT

To the extent that I haven't a cat
I am free
To the extent that I don't need
A mountain in summer
In winter a hat
I'm my own person

To the extent that I don't care for roots
I am free
To the degree that I pick my own way
Through the clutter
And sow my own oats
I am a person

But to the degree that I get to the point where I'm not
  my own person
But two of us three of us
Blurred and organic
The bond irreversible
Then I'm together

To the extent that I don't need much freedom
To do what I want
And to have what I need
And to the extent that I'm not the same person
In depth as in outline
Then I'm becoming

I think I'm allergic to absence of cat

June Siegel

THE DAY WILLIS HARDER DIDN'T
KILL HIS BEAGLE

I'm a Senior Citizen and Doctor
Rank says my chest is caving in, but
my rabbit dog's more crippled up than me.
He's so blind he gets lost in the house.
Last week I backed the truck over him.
He's deaf and he was sleeping by the lane.
I felt a bump, you know, and got out to take
a look. I could see what I done by the grass
stains on his back, so I went in to tell
the wife. "I ran over the dog," I said.
"Is he dead?" she said. I said, "Hell no."

Hilary Russell

A COW'S LIFE

I can't imagine why, or how,
A cow can bear to be a cow.

To stand all day in muck and dirt
And never get to change your shirt,

Then trudge along at someone's call
To bed down in a filthy stall,

And end up as a cut or roast of . . .
A cow's life isn't one to boast of.

I'd opt to be something more pleasant:
An osprey, maybe, or a pheasant,

An ibex, or something of that ilk,
That no one bugs for meat or milk.

Bruce Bennett

DIARY COWS

Got up early, waited for the farmer.
He hooked us all to the machines as
usual. Typical trip to the pasture,
typical trip grazing and ruminating.
About 5:00 back to the machines. What
a relief! Listened to the radio
during dinner. Lights out at 7:00.
More tomorrow.

Ron Koertge

THE CHIPMUNK CENTER

Here on the lower slopes of Windham Mountain
we have seen deer, foxes, raccoons
cheeky as pickpockets, and birds
like gold teeth among the trees. Each night
a mouse washes his mouth with soap, he's swallowed
a whole bar already: we yearn to see him smile.
But mainly, we're besieged by chipmunks, all
exactly the same size. They're born that way,
you tell me, empty beanbags with five black stripes.
Chew a few acorns and presto! instant
chipmunks, eight inches long, ready to propagate
their kind. This must be

     the chipmunk center

of the universe: they resent us
as intruders, and it's war! We've mounted
a chipmunk head above the fireplace,
its eyes swivel as we carry our bowls
of chipmunk gumbo to the table. Tiny throw rugs
cover our floor like fine handkerchiefs. We
labor all day making vests and blankets
but it's no use: their numbers swell.
This morning our car lies on its side, how
can we iron them now? We huddle together
in bed. Outside our barred windows, the red
eyes of chipmunks blaze like fireflies.

Peter Meinke

DRAWBACKS

Mosquitoes tickle with their feet
And sing off-key before they eat.
Their table manners, too, may pain you
When you're the table and the menu.

Emily Otis

LITTLE BIRDS SWOOPING

Little birds swooping
don't bother me.
What rhymes with swooping
does. And see?
I can't even say it
and still feel good.
There's always the matter
of shouldn't and should . . .
Little birds swooping
do bother me.

Mary Ann Henn

THE LAMB

He gambols to the shearer's shear
And soon his woolies disappear
And thus he gets his just deserts,
For gambolers always lose their shirts.

Bob McKenty

THE ZEBRA

A fashion tour de force
On Kenya's grassland scenes,
The zebra is a horse
Who's got designer genes.

Bob McKenty

THE MAN WHO LOVED A GIRAFFE

(*For P. B.*)

I met her on the dry plains of Samburu.
She was nibbling at a small acacia tree.
And from just a single glance there began my Great
      Romance,
For I saw she was the one giraffe for me.

Her skin was of the right reticulation.
She had the shapely figure of the young.
Her tiny horns were piquant, soft and fluffy,
And luscious was her long and purple tongue.

And her eyes! Her eyes were pools of limpid liquid
In a place where everything is sere and dried.
When she moved her silken lashes there began to rise
      new flashes
From a flame that I thought long ago had died.

We'd meet each day a little after breakfast.
She'd bend as I gazed deeply in her eyes.
We were happy on the dry plains of Samburu,
Oblivious of dust and heat and flies.

• 114

But safaris don't stay long there in Samburu,
And my safari soon was moving on.
So knowing we must part, I went to meet her
In the cool and pregnant stillness of the dawn.

I chased the shrieking monkeys from the branches
Of the tree I climbed to share our last embrace.
I suppressed a sudden shiver as I saw her muscles quiver
When she leaned to lick the salt tears from my face.

Now I ruminate on Kismet and on Kenya,
As I sit here cold and lonely in my chair.
In my mind's eye I'm sojourning in Samburu
And my undulating ungulate is there.

And you, love, midst the wildebeest and zebra,
While you cruise along the dry Samburu plain,
Have you found another guy—perhaps a rather tall
      Masai?
Will you write? Or am I doomed to wait in vain?

Pyke Johnson, Jr.

THE TURTLE

The turtle
must chortle
when he watches us.

He must think, "Well—
what's all the hustle
and the fuss?"

Mark Sanders

ANOTHER FABLE IN TWO LANGUAGES

Le Concombre Triste

J'ai connu un vieux concombre
D'un tempérament plutôt sombre;
"Triste, triste," disait-il: "C'est mon sort
De pendre à l'ombre jusqu'à la mort."

The Sorrowful Cucumber

My old friend the cucumber's soul
Was what you'd call glum, on the whole;
"My doom, too, is gloomy," he said:
"To hang in the shade until dead."

Charles W. Pratt

SHEEP THAT PASS IN THE NIGHT

It's often said that counting sheep
Will help a person fall asleep.
Attempting to resolve my doubt
About this scheme, I tried it out
And did my utmost to assign
Each sheep its tally in the line.
I muffed it, which was hard to take.
I simply couldn't stay awake
To count a fairly decent number.
I foundered, comatose in slumber.

Irene Warsaw

ZEBRAS

Zebras
    (and amoebas)
never worry
    when the bees buzz;
they just wonder
    (as the flea does)
what the cause
    of all the noise was.

Terry P. Beh

THE ACHIEVEMENTS OF HERRINGS

What can a herring do?
For deeds of derring-do
its talents are small.
But it can swim in sea
so icy-cold that we
wouldn't be choosing to,
we'd be refusing to
swim there at all!

Gavin Ewart

THE BEER AND THE BEAR

A beer is delicious, while a bear may be vicious;
    This is a difference traditional.
The head of beer consists of foam; the bear's head dreams
    of honeycomb;
    This is a difference additional.
The beer goes into people, and the people into bear;
    This is a difference nutritional.

Robert N. Feinstein

THE ANTS

Whenever one of the family entered another room,
the furniture had been rearranged.
While asleep, their beds levitated as if possessed.
Food began to disappear and the mother became tired
of scolding the cocker spaniel.

"Ghosts," the father said. The family was not so sure
of which street they lived on. Each morning,
they would wake to find their house in another part of
       town—
the mail hopelessly lost, as were the children
coming home from school.

Mark Thalman

MSSRS. MICE AND CO.*

Taking always a keen interest
in your near- and where-abouts
when it's time for you
to make your winter's nest,
I felt compelled to write you
(bless your sneaky little snouts)
a few lines to assist you in your quest.

---

* According to the *Illustrated Book of Days*, an old American remedy for ridding one's household of rats and mice was to write them a letter inviting them to go elsewhere. This letter was to be left rolled up in one of their holes.

I'll admit my pantry's cozy—
muffins, cookies, cracker crumbs
enough to blear a beady rodent eye.
Yet your future won't be rosy,
M. musculus, should you try
the larder, nor will I stand dumb
to your nibbling attempts at being nosy.

This letter's to inform you
how I intend to clean away all
morsels that could make you sleek and fat.
And apropos the mewing, it's your clue
I've made a silent partner of a cat
whose green eyes would appall
you, and whose claws you'd surely rue.

Herewith, let me refer your tails
your tummies, ears, and other parts
one block west where you'll find
a farmer's barn stacked high with bales
of hay, a corn shucker where they grind
hard kernels to sweet meal, and a smart
cow who gives sweet cream by the pail.

I shall do you no harm
should you heed my advice.
But if you foolishly try to move in,
don't count on your fuzzy charm.
Determined as I am to win,
I'd perforce buy some cruel device.
Here's hoping this note will suffice.

Mary J. McArthur

BIRD NOTES ON A BEAUTIFUL BUT NOISY APRIL MORNING

Swans mate for life and never sing,
While many a wayward bird
Releases—every public spring—
The annual male word

Common to every romeo's
And salesman's repertory:
Que je suis beau! Cueillons des roses!
And, *this is my territory* . . .

Blowing his bugle. And echoing through
Pavilioned towers of trees
To Ladies listening—listening to
A different drum (forsooth!) in these

Itinerant braggarts bruiting blind
A beauty bare about
For nestfuls of the barest kind;
These *jongleurs*—who, in rout,

Convention-bound, abandon bride,
Frau, Kinder, Küche and all
To join great swans in their quiet pride
In the silence of the fall.

Scott Bates

NUTHATCH

I've yet to see
a nuthatch
hatch a nut
but
a nuthatch
hatching
nuts would
surely also be
a nut.

Edward Coletti

DOMESTIC BIRDS

I. *The Double-Breasted Garish*

Indigenous to brass coat trees,
the Garish fans its plume—
spun paisley tail to stir a breeze
in the close sitting room.

The eye snaps catch the dusted light
from one half curtained beam,
and glisten with imagined flight,
a bright bloomed jungle dream.

II. *The Long-Tailed Tux*

Nocturnally inclined, the Long-Tailed Tux
slips from its rustling garment bag to peck
at canapes and party mix—deluxe,
in the posh serving line. A ruffled neck

of white to coax the sparkled glance of some
lush feathered debutante, the Tux glides by
on wings of cool indifference, yet one
cuff cocked to snare each whisper—every sigh.

III. *The Blue Denim*

As common as a laundry day,
the Denim lights most anywhere:
a bed post knob, the high back chair
nearest the kitchen door. The Jay,

its closest cousin, jeers away
when it swings on the line to dry.
They say old Denims never die . . .
(No need to finish that cliché.)

IV. *The Tufted Sable*

Perched on a satin hanger, royalty
among the walk-in's specimens, it eyes
its aviary mates disdainfully.

"M'lady's taste doth lapse." The Sable spies
an oblong glass beneath the hat box shelf,
and preens, and is enamored with itself.

V. *The Yellow-Billed Slicker*

Well suited yet unelegant,
the Slicker roosts inside
the cluttered pantry, well content
on sun-drenched days to bide

dank hours in the mildewed dark,
until the spring rains send

streams tripping down the gutters, and
the pond leaps in the park.

Robert Bess

BEWARE THE TIDES OF MARCH

In March the gentle zephyrs blow,
And a bright sun softens the ridges.
Spring rains mix with winter snow;
Freshets into rivers flow;
Rivers into monsters grow,
Till they're too darned big for their bridges!

Charles L. Grove

ARIES SIDESHOW

Like a magnet
under the magician's cloth,
the swan's reflection
pulls her across the lake
while deep inside the brush
an unseen hand pulls rabbits
out of rabbits.

Charles Ghigna

HAIKU

Flagstone steps:
the dog's wet paws
make flower prints

Alexis Rotella

THE NAKED EYE

On lines from Emily Dickinson's letters

The chickens grow very fast—
I am afraid they will be so large
   that you cannot perceive them
with the naked eye when you get home.

The flowers have reached the eaves
and are heaving against the roof
   which has begun to buckle—
you will have to do something I fear.

We had eggs for breakfast or,
rather, an egg—the yellow yolk
   ran under the sideboard, and
it stayed there, refusing to come out.

The cat walking down the stair
makes a great noise—the banister
   bulges out as she descends.
The trees in the yard block out the sun—

we are not sure that the sun
still regards us in our small world
   with a great eye fully clothed
in the raiment of its rays and beams.

We stumble in the shadows.
The candles speak so slightly that
   we can hardly hear their words,
and the moss—the moss is at the door.

Lewis Turco

4

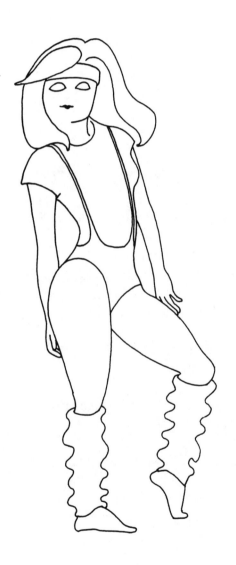

THE LIVING MASTERS

(George Barker, David Gascoyne, Gavin Ewart, billed
as such at the Royal Berkshire Poetry Festival)

Those living masters!
But suppose their living mistresses
and living boyfriends
turned up too?

A full coachload,
I reckon.

If the dead ones came along
(the sexy ghosts)
the whole lot
should fill two buses!

Gavin Ewart

Note: All three of these British poets began writing in the Thirties.

TO HIS IMPORTUNATE MISTRESS

(Andrew Marvell Updated)

Had we but world enough, and time,
My coyness, lady, were a crime,
But at my back I always hear
Time's wingèd chariot, striking fear
The hour is nigh when creditors
Will prove to be my predators.
As wages of our picaresque,
Bag lunches bolted at my desk
Must stand as fealty to you
For each expensive rendezvous.
Obeisance at your marble feet
Deserves the best-appointed suite,
And would have, lacked I not the pelf
To pleasure also thus myself;
But aptly sumptuous amorous scenes
Rule out the rake of modest means.

Since mistress presupposes wife,
It means a doubly costly life;
For fools by second passion fired
A second income is required,
The earning which consumes the hours
They'd hoped to spend in rented bowers.
To hostelries the worst of fates
That weekly raise their daily rates!
I gather, lady, from your scoffing
A bloke more solvent in the offing.
So revels thus to rivals go
For want of monetary flow.
How vexing that inconstant cash
The constant suitor must abash,

Who with excuses vainly pled
Must rue the undishevelled bed,
And that for paltry reasons given
His conscience may remain unriven.

Peter De Vries

LUCKY DILEMMA

I'd send her sweets to celebrate,
But damn those dental bills!
Most flowers make me hesitate—
Her allergy needs pills.

The jewelry I bring home won't do,
She doesn't share my taste;
High fashion for a lady who
Loves jeans is just a waste.

I cannot send a VCR,
She's not TV-inclined;
Why buy a lovely objet d'art?
The dear is color-blind!

An island cruise has no appeal—
Choppy seas upset her;
And fear of flying's an ordeal
That isn't any better.

Selecting gifts is just de trop.
Still, I'm a lucky gent:
For unlike other wives I know,
She seldom costs a cent!

Ned Pastor

ME WANTS A MINKS

Me thinks me wants a pickle.
Sometimes I wants those things.
The thing I wants me thinks,
I wants a diamond ring.
Sometimes, I wants pink roses
All different colored pinks.
But, the thing me wants the most,
Me wants a big brown minks.

E. W. Sneed

A BRIDE OF THE 80'S, DOWN THE AISLE

On the row behind her mother
sits her former live-in lover.
She also spies, across the way,
her natural daddy, now turned gay.
(Her step-dad's giving her away.)
The best man's dapper, looks elated,
he and his wife are separated,
which is o.k.—from her side, too.
She's sitting with the man in blue.
(The man in blue and the groomsman's mother
once were married to each other.)
The priest decrees that one should never
end this solemn firm endeavor,
to which all present do agree,
including the bridegroom's progeny—
so cutely dressed, so undisparaged—
products of a former marriage.

Blanche Farley

TO HAVE AND TOO OLD

The bride, white of hair, is stooped over her cane,
   Her faltering footsteps need guiding,
While down the church aisle, with a wan, toothless smile,
   The groom in a wheel chair comes riding.

And who is this elderly couple, you ask?
   You'll find, when you've closely explored it,
That here is that rare, most conservative pair,
   Who waited till they could afford it.

Richard Armour

YUPPIES VS. NOPIES

If market trends can be believed,
Then Yuppies, once ignored,
Now spend the bucks that sellers think
Most Nopies can't afford.
It's thought that Nopies, all washed up,
Just rock in chairs and hum;
I mean those Nice Old Parents whom
Most Yuppies borrow from!

Ned Pastor

TRUE LOVE

True love sticks around for more than a season,
Behaves less like a bluebird, more like a pigeon.

Wade Newman

PREGNANT THOUGHT

The male sea horse,
No ifs, buts, maybes,
Gets women's praise.
He has the babies.

Merry Harris

HORRORSCOPE

The joys of their relationship
were something less than galactical.
She was always practically perfect,
and he was perfectly practical.

John D. Engle, Jr.

THE DANGEROUS CLIFFS

"You always kill the thing you love."
So runs the curse. A
fellow gives his gal a shove
or vice versa.

Bruce Bennett

MARRIAGE COUPLET

I think of my wife. And I think of Lot,
And I think of the lucky break he got.

William Cole

VIOLA D'AMORE

"Woman is a delightful instrument, of which love is
the bow, and man the artist."

—Stendhal

She was his instrument, and oh,
How well he wielded love's bow.
At any hour, in any key,
He played with virtuosity.

But after years of harmony
She started losing her esprit,
And then her bridge began to crack . . .
He lost a screw, his bow went slack.
Her F-holes warped, her belly swelled,
She creaked whenever she was held.
His fiddling became erratic,
His technique merely automatic.
Appassionata's soon gave way
To rallentando's, then, no play.

One day he placed her on the shelf,
And humming softly to himself,
Put on his coat, and out he went
To find a better instrument.

Some may agree, with knowing smile,
That of the two, he was more viol.

Joan Van Poznak

THE RACE

He: I met my wife at the marathon;
Now I sit quietly, but she runs on.

She: At the marathon, I met my hubby;
I'm still slim, but he's grown tubby.

James Camp

BETTER REFRAIN

If I mention it twice, I'm nagging,
so—once said—I put it behind me,
ready to bet that he won't forget
to yell, "But you didn't REMIND me!"

Marian Gleason

WHO, ME?

Spontaneous is what I am,
And schedules I dread.
(This causes much dismay to Sam,
Who likes to plan ahead.)

I mean to be in harmony,
But every tune I romp to
Is—whether in or out of key—
Incredibly impromptu!

Oh, I'm as clever as a clam:
To plan I am unable.
Spontaneous is what I am!
(Sam says I am unstable.)

Hallie Hodgson

I LOVE EVERY HAIR OFF YOUR HEAD

> The facial expression associated with early baldness is
> a fixed smile, indicating hyperactivity of the occipitalis.
>
> —*Modern Medicine*

I should worry, I should care,
Give me the smile instead of the hair.
What if the price of sunny grinning
Be a progressive hirsute thinning?
What if the dictum's categoric
That hair recedes on brows euphoric?
What if your pate grows more bereft?
You'll still have me and a few wisps left.
A sourpuss, frowning with ennui,
Can fondle his wave, but not fondle me.

Alma Denny

NO MUSE IS GOOD MUSE

To be an Artist you need talent, as well as a wife
who washes the socks and the children,
and returns phone calls and library books and types.
In other words, the reason there are so many more
Men Geniuses than Women Geniuses is not Genius.
It is because Hemingway never joined the P.T.A.
And Artur Rubinstein ignored Halloween.
Do you think Portnoy's creator sits through children's
          theater
matinees—on Saturdays?
Or that Norman Mailer faced 'driver's ed' failure,
chicken pox or chipped teeth?
Fitzgerald's night was so tender because the fender
his teen-ager dented happened when Papa was at a story
          conference.

Since Picasso did the painting, Mrs. Picasso did the toilet
	training.
And if Saul Bellow, National Book Award winner, invited
	thirty-three
for Thanksgiving Day dinner, I'll bet he had help.
I'm sure Henry Moore was never a Cub Scout leader,
and Leonard Bernstein never instructed a tricycler
On becoming a bicycler just before he conducted.
Tell me again my anatomy is not necessarily my destiny,
tell me my hang-up is a personal and not a universal
	quandary,
and I'll tell you no muse is a good muse
unless she also helps with the laundry.

Rochelle Distelheim

FOUR LETTER WORDS

The lowest in my book:
WASH, IRON, MEND, and COOK.

Stella Moss

SOME ITALIAN!

(to be read with a thick accent)

I thought all it took to cook Italian
was big hips and bare feet.

Too proud for a colander,
I trusted potholders so new they no bend
to hold an upside-down pot and the lid

just crooked enough
to spill out boiling water,
scalding my hand and sending spaghetti
sliding down the drain before you could say
pasta fagioli. That night I lay sideways
on my big hip with my hand
in a big pan of cold water.

Now I shake in my bare feet
at the sight of big pots.
Boiling only in saucepans,
I discovered my specialty:
spaghetti carbonizzati al Ragu.

Set a fistful in a pan
so it leans against the rim
like a seasaw with nobody on it.
(Forget the protruding sticks.)
When you smell the edges curling over
and falling onto the burner,
remove pan to sink,
grabbing tongs and scissors.
(At this point I usually stub my big toe.)
The cutting of the burnt ends
takes about five minutes.
Return pan to burner and allow to boil
for an *arbitrario* amount of time.
Spaghetti of wormlike texture mixed
with the burnt bits that fall in
makes a succulent dish (if you not picky).

Eh! Maybe it takes being barefoot
and pregnant.

Linda Monacelli Johnson

SPONGE

I never feel the slightest guilt
At crying over milk that's spilt.
If I cry long and loud enough,
Someone just might mop up the stuff!

Maureen Cannon

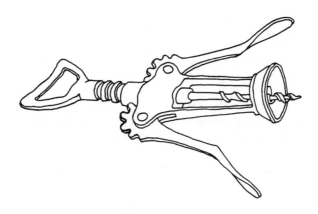

AT HOME

After thirty-five years more
or less side by side
they ride out another
evening, she like
a marble table
squared upon the carpet,
he a padded armchair
crookedly
sagging.

Edward Willey

SEQUENCE

The nocturnal life
Of a man and his wife
This pattern quite often assumes:
First two in a bed,
Then each in a bed,
Then sleeping in separate rooms.

Richard Armour

AFFLUENCE

Your ample house has amplified your plight.
The wife who sang once, charmed you, seemed so right
is now a toilet flushing in the night.

Richard Moore

Q.E.D.

"Nobody's perfect," she said,
As she tumbled in over her head.
He replied, as she sank out of sight,
"My dear, you are perfectly right."

Laurence Perrine

THE NEW COURTSHIP

Locked at last in our last embrace,
the struggle over who gets what,
we sense our passion grow too hot
to meet each other face-to-face.

Now lawyers represent our rages,
and of our hate the final scenes
are carried out by go-betweens—
like love scenes in the Middle Ages.

Richard Moore

PORTRAIT

Bobby Newly,
Rough, unruly,
Scared the girls
With funny faces.

Now he's older,
None the wiser,
And scares the ladies
With grim grimaces.

Dick Hayman

JENNIFER BLASS

A difficult lass is Jennifer Blass.
They say when she's out on a date
She orders her steak in a water glass
Her milk on a dinner plate.
As soon as it's brought she smacks her lips
And while the waiter glowers
She drinks her steak in little sips
And chews her milk for hours.

Mildred Luton

PREPOSTEROUS

At fifteen Jean Calvin made a list:
Best Legs, Sexiest Smile, Best Muscles,
all the rest. She had the right to judge us
since she was Most Buxom herself,
Most Dreamed About,
Most Discussed When Flesh Came Up.

I sat behind her in Civics that aromatic year
and whispered jokes and tried to breathe her hair.
For all that I won Wittiest. Wittiest.
And was runner-up for Best Legs on a Short Boy.

She posted it and overnight her picks
for All-round Sexiest, Perkiest Buns, Dreamiest,
drew flocks around their lockers.
And everything I said was suddenly preposterous
and clever. I could roll my eyes that June
and break up Biology.

It wasn't what I wanted, but I took it.
I wanted to be one of those who could whisper
in Jean Calvin's hair and make her wheel and slap
and turn back around with a secret smile.
I wanted a gift: Best Voice, Bedroomiest Eyes,
some arousing inherited trait. Not this,
this Wittiest, which makes me work so hard,
so everlastingly, to keep Jean Calvin entertained.

Jim Hall

ADVICE AGAINST THUMBERS

Beware of the ones with red lips
and training bras. For a six-pack
they will show you their knobby knees,
for a joint they will hike their skirts
up to their thighs. They will blow
smoke rings in your face and chew gum
and offer you none. They will say
they were born in Denver at the age
of twelve, and other funny things.
They will bad-mouth Marylou
for copping out at the drive-in,
the crumb bum. They will jab you
with an elbow on a sharp turn
and slip their braces from their teeth
just when they know you're looking.
They will call you Mister and say
you look like Omar Sharif.
They will drive your adrenalin
and other juices in motion,
and say they are off to the woods
to find Goldilocks and friends, ha-ha.
Beware, beware. They will memorize
your license plate numbers and lift
your fingerprints off the dashboard.
They will leave hairpins on your carpet,
lipstick on your seat belts and a note
to be found by your wife or lover,
beginning, "Dear Wive or Luver . . . "

Harold Bond

INVITATION

"Will you walk with me,
  Miss Walker?"
Says Miss Walker,
  "Well, I might."
"Will you run with me,
  Miss Walker?"
Says Miss Walker,
  "Not tonight."
"Will you skip with me,
  Miss Walker?"
Says Miss Walker,
  "No, I won't."
"Will you leap with me,
  Miss Walker?"
Says Miss Walker,
  "Sensible people don't leap—
  but *I* will."

James Steel Smith

HAT TRICK

When Henry kissed Heather,
His cap grew a feather,
Although the encounter was brief;

And then he met Lonnie,
And hey-nonny-nonny,
She made him an Indian chief.

Paul Humphrey

TRIOLET, AFTER TITIAN

To think when Diet made my lover less
that I should love her more
seems an affront to Venus' opulent undress.
To think when Diet made my lover less
there than Venus, there too, I guess,
than rosy Venus in the arms of War,
to think when Diet made my lover less
that I should love her more!

Sylvester Pollet

SILK PYJAMAS

Life doesn't offer much better
than silk pyjamas
unless
it's red silk pyjamas.

Red silk pyjamas stand higher
than anything
except
embossed red silk pyjamas.

Silky, textured, red pyjamas
surpass everything.
Almost.
I forgot two lovers sharing one pair of red silk pyjamas.

Michael Holstein

HONEYMOON IN NICE

The third day of our honeymoon
She woke with a guileless whim
To see the town and shop alone.
I could enjoy a swim.

Tossing her head, she looked so free,
I had no cause to doubt her,
But I damned the palms and azure sea
After an hour without her.

Francis J. Smith

LOVE-DEEP IN CROSSWORD PUZZLES

Love-deep in crossword puzzles,
Young couples sit apart.
Son of Ruth—Obed.
Eyebrow—Bree.
Changsa is the Capital of Hunan.
The sun falls vertical.
Everyone in the park is chewing a pencil.
Nobody erases.
Most write with ink.
The President of the United States has declared an
      embargo on clues.
Spain cannot withstand the blockade on Crossword
      Puzzles.
Soon we will be at war.
Generals are doing the same puzzles twice.
But what is going to happen to me?
I have none of the answers.
Daphnis' lover is Chloe.

Ridd is the husband of Lorna Doone.
It is time to count the two-lettered gods.
I didn't buy a paper.
I don't have a puzzle to do.
Light spreads horizontal
& the trees are lost in thought.

Louis Phillips

IN PRAISE OF SOBRIETY

"Lips that touch liquor must never touch mine." That's
    clear.
And yet they still keep trying. And come near.
But, with a tipsy lunge, hit nose or ear.

John Frederick Nims

FOR A GOOD OLE BOY

Vodka. Grapefruit juice. In paper cups.
Life discussed among abandoned graves.
Later outside a diner when you threw up,
I finally understood why JESUS SAVES.
Like you'd save me. But Mama knew best—
It's her you'll sleep with is my guess.
But this spring you escape the tomb;
Ride; drink beer; watch dogwoods bloom.

Mary Veazey

THINGS AS THEY ARE

Sometimes things as they are
pack up their jeans
and jump in the car
and drive halfway to New Orleans

before you realize they're
gone and what you got is a broom
in one hand, a baby in the other
and some guy who wants to rent the room

and the guy looks familiar—
coal-eyed, been
drivin all night he says and wonders
would you take him in
and you take him in

Bonnie Jacobson

AIRPORT PHONE BOOTH

All those men who couldn't live without me,
did.
I see their faces
as I travel through their cities.
If I telephoned,
intelligent children would answer,
cool wives would wait
at perfect dining tables,
and deep, polite voices
would be fine, how am I?

Memye Curtis Tucker

ELEGY FOR THE OTHER WOMAN

May her plane explode
with just one fatality.
But, should it not,
may the other woman spew
persistent dysentery from
your first night ever after.
May the other woman vomit
African bees and Argentine wasps.
May cobras uncoil from her loins.
May she be eaten not
by something dramatic like lions,
merely by a wart-hog.
I do not wish the other woman
to fall down a well
for fear of spoiling the water,
nor die on the highway because
she might obstruct traffic.
Rather: something easy, and cheap,
like clap from some other bloke.
And should she still survive
all these critical possibilities,
may she quietly die of boredom with you.

Elisavietta Ritchie

THE BIG BANG

"You were in my dream a couple of nights ago."
She gave him a steady look, and said "I know."

Howard Nemerov

TWO WOMEN

I. LORRAINE

I want to tell you in advance I eat
other things besides strawberries
and melons, but not by choice. I force
myself to eat what's green, asparagus
and broccoli. I know what's good
for me. It's your respect I want,
not your desire. You think I'm
the one who buys red bras and
wears them. But you could talk
to me of Baudelaire and Job.
You think I can't plot a graph.
Where do you get off? I lift
my own duffel. I'm no helpless
calico. I'm spiritual.

Last night I scratched my cornea,
that's why this black patch
on my eye. But I'm no one-eyed
Jack. I see what's going on.
She's young and sullen, not
your type. Poke her with a cattle
prod, she'll drag her bloated butt
behind. Now me, I climb high diving
boards, slice water like a knife
through brie. I can make you melt,
baby, or be cool as ice. Either
way, I didn't pack this red bra
for nothing.

II. RUTH

I don't know what it's like to be
beautiful, I only know this sorrow
which some men find bountiful.
I could tell you of men who
offer themselves like tin cups.
They scratch the dirt my footprints
leave. They have no shame, they
squat. I had a lover once to whom
I gave my lips, all smoldering
because he harbored sorrow too
and I will tell you what it was
like: randy. Moss and moist and
verdant. We were sucked in,
floundering, to that pious
place of tears, where dragonflies
swarm with phosphorescent wings.

Barbara Goldberg

THE RAKE'S PROGRESS

Now he's older and less virile
he'll settle down with some nice girile.

Vonna Adrian

THE PASSIONATE BUSINESSMAN TO HIS LOVE

Come live with me and be my love—
Or, better yet, let's meet
Clandestinely, at intervals
Convenient and discreet.

Bruce Bennett

(914) 555-4144

Clare was cute but crabby, clannish;
Maud was much too mod and mannish.
Doris—dimpled, shapely, vain-ish—
Lived on yogurt, coffee, Danish.
Bossy Betty, quite a tall dish,
Fell for someone short and baldish.
Fickle Florence, warm then coolish,
Loved me, left me—oh how foolish!
Sue, who loved to ski, was skittish;
Yetta bent my ear in Yiddish.
Here I am—still single, sporty—
Call me if you're under forty!

Ned Pastor

MOLLY GAUNT

Hell was real for Molly Gaunt,
Everybody's maiden aunt.
She'd always heard that love was sin,
So shunned the fire and burned within.
She guarded close her virgin state
Until her death at eighty-eight;
But nonetheless she went to Hell.
     Ah, well!
That's the way with maiden aunts.
Honi soit qui mal y pense.

H. Wendell Smith

RONDINE OF THE RARE DEVICE

"If You Can Kiss the Mistress, Never Kiss the Maid."
from *A Collection of English Proverbs*, 1678.

The maid will do if you are not ambitious—
Why split the stalk if twigs will make the besom?
Why kill the roots if one may steal the blossom?
The garden is a plot of sundry pleasures,
Filled with winding paths and rare devices,
Here a fountain, there a Grecian column—
    The maid will do.

Rose O'Morning winds upon the trellis,
All hips and nettles, snags and lures at random.
Is desire the better part of wisdom?
Brown-eyed Susan smiles from her bed of grasses—
    The maid will do.

Wesli Court

CHALLENGES

My boarder's new girl, a zippy brunette,
looks me over as I emerge
from the cellar.

Although I have lived here 23 years
and carried 23 X 365 loads
of laundry up these dim steps,

tonight my arms only hold
a bottle of elderly wine
and two silver goblets.

My boarder is younger than
my own son, yet strangely I sense
his girlfriend senses a rival.

My hair and my teeth
are my own and my stockings
are black, and lace.

"And who are you?" she demands.
"What's your function here
in this crazy place?"

I ponder her question, then
look her square:
"I run this establishment."

Elisavietta Ritchie

THE BREASTS OF WOMEN

Some men would gladly die
for the big ones.

Some women would gladly kill
such men.

I say
what is, is big.

David Kirby

DARLENE FRIENDSHIP'S BOYFRIEND

got all dressed up for his 25th high school reunion
and when he got there his mind got all dressed up,
began prowling the crowded Holiday Inn banquet room
like a character in the opening pages of a short story,
carefully breaking only windows that needed breaking,
doing everything he never allowed himself to do
twenty-five years before and still without children
or a wife, mysterious all night long without explanation,
affixing his signature to the everything of things
easily and without malice like a virgin might in his
own rightful name and in the name of Darlene
        Friendship.

Ron Ikan

WALKING NAKED AROUND THE HOUSE

Walking naked around the house
I ease up to a window and look out:
the trees have their bark on,
the cats fur, dogs hair;
sparrows cruise through the air, feathered.
Even the ants which I can't actually see
scurry about orderly in their proper armor.
My wife drives up in her suede-and-raccoon coat.
I slip over to the clothes closet, logically.

R. P. Dickey

THE FAMILY IN THE SUBURBS:
A SITUATION COMEDY

1.

She bursts in on him
in the frigid garage, tools
hanging straight as a plumbline
from the pegboard,
screwdrivers, drill bits and wrenches
of every size, Toro mower
and snow blower side by side
behind the nine-passenger wagon.
Clad only in loincloth
and L. L. Bean hunting jacket
he's sitting on his haunches eating
a squirrel, blood-drops
red as cherries steaming in his beard,
bits of entrails, gristle and fur
stuck between teeth.
Women from some other side of town

dance and chant around him
dressed in the latest fashions
from Frederick's of Hollywood,
simulated-leather teddies and peek-a-boo bras,
spiked heels, garter belts, fishnet hose,
their hair wild as untrimmed rosebushes
and matted with sweat, mouths
slack with panting, lips swollen,
eyes smoldering like cigarette-tips
in a honky-tonk just before closing.
"I can explain everything," he says.

2.

Lately he's spent much of his time
in the garage, hammering, sawing, screwing
things. She takes baths.
One day her groans call him
into the house. He smashes
into the room with the ball-peen hammer
he bought at Sears that very morning,
splintering the door just as the doll
squeezes from between her thighs
and floats on its back in the steamy bathwater.
"Mama, Dada," it coos, each syllable
a bubble round as this earth
bearing heavenward their image together
and flames of the three scented K-Mart candles
blazing in their tiny cups on the back
of the commode.
"You're probably the father," she tells him,
"I swear it on my mother's grave."
"It has our eyes!" he cries.

David Citino

SOUTHERN GOTHIC

An ivory magnolia flower, with a full
cup of rain water—weighing just the same
as an iron dumbbell—fell in its full
glory on a Southern belle, who in her blame-

less beauty was crossing campus, and that fool
flower was so heavy, it snuffed out her flame
or to put it plainly, death being no fool
the only thing left of her is her name.

I come not to moralize, nor do I fool
with platitude, nor do I cry a shame.
A beauty, full, fell on the beautiful:
which beautiful is beautifully to blame.

Rodger Kamenetz

BEVERLY CARNEIRO*

She's nothing more than the grassy waist of Kansas—
still, her head lies 23 miles from her feet.

Caught up with broken incubators and second mortgages
the farmers have forgotten how to touch her, so she
    drowses

through the seasons. Sprawled across three counties
each part of her wheat-colored body dreams it's
    something else:

* Towns in Kansas. On I-70, a big green sign says:

Beverly	Carneiro
← 11	12 →

her eyes, blue herons shaking mud from their ankles;
her toes, pigs dozing through a fantasy of truffles;

blond hay on her arms, black briers in her crotch.
Massaging her spine in his father's giant tractor

a gawky boy feels new warmth rise through the seat, and
    starts
to hum a polka, but her ears are stuffed with alfalfa. And
    you,

hunched on your motorcycle, cruise over her like a fruit
    fly
crazed by a wind scented with fresh milk and apple butter.

Shift down a gear: meadowlarks flutter from finger to
    finger.
Shift down another: green lizards bask on a granite
    knuckle.

As you curve off the highway and ease down the ramp
of her collarbone into the shadow of whitewashed barns

it seems possible to love this landscape for what it's not:
it's more than earth, you're less than human, and both

are evolving fast. Abandoning the bike you begin
running along a nameless dirt road. Dust flies up

behind you, her ripe belly undulates in green heat
as you pant beneath a flock of geese veeing homeward.

Over the next hill an immense marsh simmers: closing
    in,
out of breath, you kick off your boots to feel

damp grass underfoot, as if you alone had discovered
what makes ponies toss their heads as they canter,

as if you were no temporarily crazed tourist but a goose
singing the same name these geese sing, your voice

growing simpler and surer, head sleeker, arms prickling
with feathers, shoulders already iridescent with flight.

Robert Hill Long

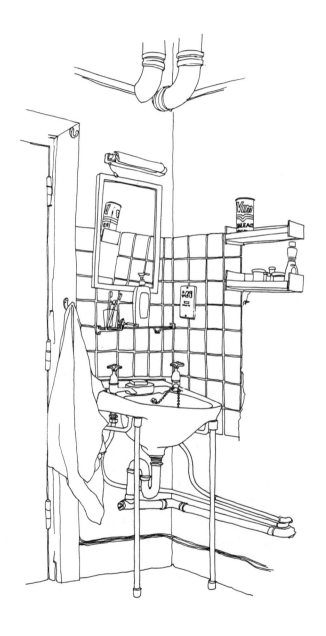

5

WHERE TO SPEND THE WINTER

One man goes north to ski.
Another south to swim.
A third stays home to read
Of snow or tropic sea.
A fourth of whom I've read
In winter goes to bed,
In other words, to beast.
His wife must wait on him.
A fifth man dies, goes west,
Or shall we say to seed?
Who knows who chooses best?

Robert Francis

GROUNDED

My aircraft lingers at its gate
Awaiting clearance, running late.
Hold, JFK; hang on, O'Hare.
My plans are all that's in the air.

Alice P. Stein

FOLLOW YOUR HEART TO THE LAND
OF ENCHANTMENT

(The Small Print on the Back of the Tour Brochure)

All prices, places, means of conveyance,
colors of ink, the paper of this brochure
and the English language itself
are subject to be changed, terminated,
doubled, tripled, incarcerated,
desecrated, or elevated to the status of gods.

The tour agent reserves the right
to rub mustard in the touree's hair,
abandon him in the desert or dessert,
or force him to sleep on a mattress
full of machine parts.

The agent reserves the right to change
the touree's mother's name without notice,
enter the touree as a horse in a steeplechase,
or break his nose with a loaf of French bread.

Make sure your deposit check is signed. No refunds.

Tom Hawkins

ARLES, 7 P.M.

Shoals of Americans scout supper,
flashing silver speed darting in the sidestreets,
faces green with low blood sugar,
follow the leader through squares lined with restaurants
all closed, all locked.
A busboy sweeping the sidewalk is sighted,
surrounded like a foreign correspondent
back from the front.
When O when do you open?

At eight o'clock finally seated
I am waiting for supper.
At eight thirty the menu makes its appearance,
long contemplated outside, memorized,
the seventy franc special drooled on, but
no the proper moment has not come
to take the order, for the moment
of order taking must ripen like cheese
put away to mold in mountain caves.

At nine o'clock the order is taken,
waiting, waiting for supper.
At nine fifteen the waiter returns,
tonight there is no John Dory,
John Dory gone down with all hands lost.
Anything else, a fried mouse, please!
roast plucked tourist under glass
stewed gendarme on blanched greenbacks
while waiting, waiting for supper.

The waiter looks delicious with
his sleeves slightly rolled.
He flees past our table, but I am
eyeing a chihuahua. If I had

a tidbit to entice him
I'd eat it, and him.
This napkin is a little starchy
but goes down with salt,
waiting, waiting for supper.

At nine thirty the bread comes.
At nine thirty five it is all eaten.
Waiting, waiting for supper.
At ten o'clock the soup arrives,
the basic Mediterranean fish soup
I make myself in half the time I have
been sitting here and I drink it
slurp slurp and it is gone.
Waiting, waiting for supper.

At half past ten the lamb arrives
and at ten thirty five I crunch the last bone,
the potatoes, the salad, vanished
into the maw of a hunger that
could yawn and devour Arles, I
Kali, Gargantua, Godzilla
on a feeding frenzy biting
into domes crunch like spun sugar,
chewing stones and plaster, chomping trees.

If I ate your city, that
would teach you to leave me here
waiting, waiting for supper.
Ah, eleven. Food finally tucked in.
Now comes the bill.
Now comes the indigestion.
Travel is broadening. In a matter
of hours we start
waiting for breakfast.

Marge Piercy

SAILING, SAILING

(Lines written to keep the mind off incipient seasickness)

There is no impeding
That proceeding,
No deflating
That undulating
Or overthrowing
The to-and-froing
Or undoing
The fro-and-toing,
That silky insisting
Never desisting,
That creasing, uncreasing
Never ceasing,
No deterrence
To the recurrence,
No cessation
To the pulsation,
No stopping the dropping
Of the wave,
The plopping, slopping
Of the foam.
We brave it
Afloat in a boat
On the perpetual
Wet-you-all
(No controlling that rolling)
Motion
Hasten, Jason
Of the ocean.
Get the basin.

Lillian Morrison

THE OBLIGATION

The last double scotch is consumed and the cigarettes put
    out.
We are belted into our seats as the giant jet
manufactures a louder noise for the long descent,
reminding us all of what has been holding us up.
We trust we are safe in the captain's capable hands.
We know he is there; he gave us the weather report.

We should all be grateful now for the skill of the captain.
He has taken our lives in his hands. He has landed us
    safely.
As we gather our coats we should sing out praise for the
    captain.
We should urge the officials to give him a hero's
    welcome.

The poet is especially ready to acknowledge the hero.
The poet has lectures to give, he has poems to read,
and he wants to complete the lines he has only just
    started.
He is writing a poem on the plane and its capable
    captain:
the captain is the flat voice that announces the weather,
and the captain is the hero whose heart has guided the
    ship.

Aware once again that the wings have been held in place,
the poet is glad for a chance to complete his poem,
and he tentatively hopes for another thirty-five years.
As he strides purposefully into the captain's weather,
we must all be obliged that the captain is such a hero.
He has taken the poet to his heart and landed him safely.

Knute Skinner

TUNNEL VISION

In Dover too did Kubla Khan
A stately pleasure-dome decree,
From where the Channel Tunnel ran
Through caverns hollowed out by man
To France, across the sea.

So umpteen miles of fertile ground
With concrete walls were girdled round,
And buildings rose, like dark satanic mills,
To house the vast emporia (all duty-free);
And here were florists, coffee-shops and grills
And parking lots with tubs of greenery.

But in a vision I foresaw
The plan contained one fatal flaw.

As I in pensive mood was lying
I heard ancestral voices crying
From afar: "Beware! Beware!
Not one of you who enters there
Can hope to re-emerge alive;
    You'll close your eyes in holy dread
    As half-way through you see ahead
The point where left- meets right-hand drive!"

David Cram

THE STONES OF FLORENCE

If everybody had a horse
the streets would not be clean, of course.

In fact, you'd have to hold your nose
and wash your sandals with a hose

which, while unpleasant, could be worse;
for instance, you'd avoid the curse

of being struck by something teeny
or flattened by a Lamborghini.

Bruce Bennett

MISFORTUNE'S DARLINGS

At cocktail parties they serve us
sheep dip with a choice of crackers.
Three of our major appliances
are wanted for murder.
The children we've put up
have all turned sour.
The house has a bad case of shingles.
My roses will not knuckle under.
Your leisure suit won't work anymore.
The hi-fi is playing around.
Even the cat has lost her tail.

But the picture is changing:
in the odd lots of life
we've drawn "a vacation for 2
in the Black Forest,"
where we can take the waters
at Bad Karma.

L. L. Zeiger

GUIDE TO PARIS: EIFFEL TOWER, VERSAILLES

From the top of this phallus
You can see to the palace
Which, with the blessing of Jesus
And plenty of class,
King Louis Quatorze
And his whores built for picnics
Out of nothing but peasants
And pieces of glass.

Scott Bates

UP FAIR KILTIES!

Wee kilties in the bonnie breese,
waft highe to shew wa' hang;
ere wa' not Fruity Loom to see,
but ruddy Auld Syne lang!
    wi' a wang, a wang!

Aye, we pipe a highland dittie,
and wunder wat'le gang;
we consider it a pittie,
such endowments are ni' sang!
    wi' a wang, a wang!

So rise up, and lift, fair Murdoch,
for all of us to see;
looks like thistle or a burdock,
and fills us all wi' glie!
    wi' a wang, wang!

O it kinna be slight hairbell,
and nai bluebell ging 'ding-dong!';
and pipes make Scottie harts swell,
contraire to this wee dongh!
      wi' a wang, a wang!

So we strait to battle blunder,
bright coombs and blades adrout;
wi' nai wurrie what's hereunder,
as 'piz on you!' we shout!
      wi' a wang, a wang!

Now olde spoutes spit
ye biled streams forth,
steam billoes wi' dreer thunder;
for ne'er did 'ere
the Tartan Werth,
wrought miracles down under!
      wi' a wang, a wang!

O'er battle sounds of burnde and drownde,
wi' spirits and kilties a' flyin',
'mid woonded and dunne,
we howled at the sonne,
"We'll fug iny bugger not dyin'!"
      wi' a ding and a dingle,
      a dingle and dong,
      and a wang!
      a wang!

Russ Traunstein

SAFFRON PIG PIÑATA

Look at me standing
on one foot and a crutch
in the Mexico City airport
eating a stuffed zucchini
with a Paris surgeon
and necrophiliac
of no little renown. Would you
care, he asked,
to join me and some
acquaintenances for a little
get-together this weekend
at my chateau in Pseudo-Nantes.

Why not, I answered, noticing
the mayhem of ragweed pollen
dusting his cape, like a party
of fireflies in a boneyard
after a cholera epidemic. Are you
a vegetarian, he inquired?
                    Perspiring
from the tea, winding sheets of dry
Dutch cigar smoke and a ticklish
memory of my grandfather separating
from his body, like a hermit
crab racing from one shell
to another, I replied,
have you heard the one
about the saffron pig?

Roger Weingarten

HEARTBREAK IN TUKTOYAKTUK

> "The longest Inuvialuktun word that linguists have
> identified is a bit of a jawbreaker. It is 'tuktusiuria-
> gatigitqingnapin'ngitkiptin'nga.' Translation: 'You'll
> never go caribou hunting with me again.' "
>
> Christopher Wren, The New York *Times* (July 9,
> 1985)

How many times has it been sd. in jest:
Tuktusiuriagatigitqingnapin'ngitkiptin'nga?
But when you turned to me & sd:
Tuktusiuriagatigitqingnapin'ngitkiptin'nga,
There was no laughter on your lips.
I sd. "Huh? Could you repeat that slowly?"
But, of course, you couldn't,
& so we have continued our hunt for Caribou,
Tho, of course, it isn't quite the same
Ever since you tried to say to me
Tuktusiuriagatigitqingnapin'ngitkiptin'nga.

Louis Phillips

TALLYHO THE FOX

In America, riding to hounds
No longer abounds.
In fact, like fishing for squid,
It never did.

Louis Hasley

HOME, SWEET HOME!

"The cyanide—it was put in her tea—didn't reach Mrs. Shaw, but killed a house-cat."

—Ellery Queen, *The Adventure Of The Bearded Lady*

The American Language explicates everything—
a guest is a house-guest, a cat is a house-cat;
but every coat isn't a house-coat
nor every boat a house-boat.
You *could* have a house-mouse or a house-rat
but not a house-condor or a house-shark.
However much wildness and inexactitude are hated
not *everything* can be domesticated.

Gavin Ewart

LIMERICKS

In the place where I live the worst irritants
Are some elderly puritan militants
Who think wine, women and song
Are terribly wrong;
We call them the Local Inhibitants.

*

There was an explorer called White
Who was English, and over-polite.
When a cannibal ate him
(And I quote him verbatim)
He died saying: "Good appetite!"

David Cram

A grumpy old owl at the zoo,
Hearing other birds' soft bill and coo,
    Hooted, "Silly chit-chit!
    Just *listen* to it!
Thank god, I've more wit than to woo!"

*

A graduate student's faux-pas
Made her throw up her hands and say, "Psha!
    Well, it happens to myriads—
    I'm missing my periods.
Instead of M.A. I'll be 'Ma!' "

*

A stammerer, loving to roam,
Making conquests from Key West to Nome,
    Pausing once in his life
    To remember his wife,
Said, "I must be-be-getting back home!"

*

For beauty the swan takes the crown:
On a river where others would drown,
   She floats like a dream
   Eider down- or upstream,
And what bears her up is her down.

*

An erudite scholar of Mich-
elangelo, Braque, and Van Dyke
   Confessed, "For my part,
   I know all about art,
But I no longer know what I like."

*

The pretty twins, Lottie and Lou,
I shyly had long wished to woo,
   When, intent to assist me,
   They suddenly kissed me.
I confessed, "I've long wanted you { to." / too." / two."

Laurence Perrine

SHE DON'T BOP

A nervous young woman named Trudy
Was at odds with a horn player, Rudy.
His horn so annoyed her
The neighbors would loiter
To watch Rudy toot Trudy fruity.

Keith Casto

QUAIL

There's a story about a young quail
Who was sad because she had no tail.

She tried out her luck,
Wrote to Sears & Roebuck,
And had one delivered by mail.

Katharyn Machan Aal

OFFICE HOURS

A student who wanted an A
Went up to his teacher to say,
"Can we meet tonight
So I'll get it right,
The difference between *lie* and *lay?*"

Katharyn Machan Aal

WELL BED

Said the matron to pretty Miss Whytal,
"In Boston, good breeding is vytal!"
"In The Bronx, it is too,"
Miss Whytal did coo,
"But it's known by a different tytal!"

Lola Strong Janes

RIBALD RIVER RHYME

Sailing on the Gulf of Oman
I got to thinking about Onan;
I knew the Bible had forbid it
But anyway I went and did it.

William Cole

THE WONDERFUL WORLD

In Disneyland, you have to search
to find a toilet.
There's one on Main Street, U.S.A.,
and one among the South Sea Island shops.
But woe betide you in Tomorrowland
or out on yesterday's Frontier.
It's as though toilets were added
    as an afterthought—
something not needed in a world so clean,
with patrolling regiments of close-cropped boys
snapping up dirt with dustpan-brooms.
Why, even the horses pulling Main Street cars
    know how to hold it in.

Robert D. Sutherland

ATTIC DANCE

To the music of the guzla
light-foot Grecian ladies amble
through the maze of the romaika
for the pleasure of their lords.
And they find they're growing fonder
of the rhythm of the guzla
and the moves of the romaika,
all those leisure-loving lords.
And the guzla thrumming louder,
the romaika steps go faster
as the bare feet of the ladies
flash below their skirts of gauze.
As they raise brown arms, their bangles

make a sweet and tuneful clangor
and their lords rise up and join them
on the green and trampled sward.
On they whirl in fierce abandon,
clasp hot hands and dance in tandem
to the music of the guzla,
through the maze of the romaika
on the flower-scented sward,
every lady with her lord.

Joan Drew Ritchings

A LUST FOR THE QUAINT OLD WAYS

an acrostic

My favorite spot of all is home
In the warm sheath of bed,
Snug. More adventuresome types roam,
Sampling, experimenting, always led
In odd directions by a passion to get
On in the world. Either it's the crannies and
Nooks of the Amazon they have a taste for, let
Attract them south, or else the northern land
Rules their desires, their prows devoured by
Yawning fiords. Not so I:

Zeal for my little house consumes me,
Excessively perhaps, but burning steadfast
Always with a cozy flame; free
Lubriciousness for this homely enthusiast.

John J. Brugaletta

POEM FOUND WHILE I LOOKED FOR SOMETHING ELSE

In southern Chinese
Fuking means
Happiness Capital:
wise these
Chinese.

Joseph DeRoller

LAS VEGAS

Hens inch in Mustangs, cluck
to cocks to sink their shots,
and cinch their gambling luck,
in private, two-armed slots.

Ernest Kroll

MITZI

There was a young lady named Mitzi
Who was diagnosed as a schitzy.
With loud cries of glee,
She would publicly pee
In such clubs in New York
As Larue and the Stork
And hotels like the Waldorf and Ritzi.

Weldon Kees

BOVINE TOWN

If you should chance to meet a cow
in Jumpoff, Tennessee
take off your hat and make a bow
and ask her how she be,
for Jumpoff is a mountain town
where cows have ruled for years.
The mayor is a Hereford bull.
The aldermen are steers
and if your manners aren't polite
they'll chase you off the square.
If you are not a cow yourself
you've little business there.

Mildred Luton

THE OFFICIAL FRISBEE-CHASING CHAMPION
OF COLORADO

The Navajo word for *unleaded* was not
the most absurd thing on my mind
that arid evening as we rolled
into the fever-colored hills
of Monument Valley: I had been
scaring my five months pregnant wife
with a *Reader's Digest* real life horror
—a Mormon sedan broke down in the desert,
summer, the whole godfearing family
having to chew melted crayons, tire rubber,
drink each other's piss and finally
slaughter their old chihuahua—
and now, with the fuel tank's *empty* signal
lighting up like a bad cowboy-movie-sunset,

I was sorry for passing Last Chance
This and Last Chance That,
but sorry was not enough, I needed
a minor miracle and I got three:
all of them Navajo and not a one
over eight years old, chasing
a bald truck tire across the highway,
slapping it wobbly as if it were
a sick black goat or a priest caught
buying tequila with last Sunday's tithes.
I hit the brakes and jumped out
onto the twilight asphalt, shouting
—my wife hissed "Be nice!"—shouting
"Over here, I need to show you
something!" The car shuddered slightly
and died. The Navajo kids edged up
suspiciously and why not: I was
the only gringo around and I was tearing
through the back seat mess for a camera,
they probably thought, but what
was to prevent me from swinging around
with a knife and adding three more scalps
to the annals of genocide?
But it was a frisbee I produced,
the old worthless-trinket-trick
with a twist: a whistle behind it
was our old hound who (I lied)
was the unofficial frisbee-chasing
champion of Colorado.
And despite his broken teeth
and hips that shimmied with arthritis
he put on a world-class display,
snatching sand-skimmers, long range bombs,
kicking up his bad legs like a puppy
and fetching that orange disk back to me

like it was a sun he wouldn't let sink
until everyone agreed to make his title
official. Which we did amid much
ceremonious laughter and chatter,
trading names, quick stories,
all the invisible commerce of friendship.
They touched my wife's ripening belly,
pointed to a butte glowing in last light:
"The first people were born up there."
The desert was stealing our shadows
while we talked. I asked my tourist favor:
the oldest said if we pushed the car
a little way, there was a hill
curving down to a Texaco. For thanks
I gave them the frisbee and the young one asked
"Can we keep the dog too?" Was this
how disappointment came into the world,
an easy question chasing a hard answer
into the darkness? The dog sat grinning
with exhaustion, my wife winced
and looked away. Shadows bigger
than any of us were listening as I knelt
and looked into the boy's black-bean eyes:
"That dog's not worth ten dollars—
he'll die in a year. Let me buy
him back for five." He understood.
A minute later as the car glided downhill
I thought five dollars was cheap
ransom for such a narrow escape
from bitterness. I let out a whoop
and imagined cowboy harmonica music
swelling over the whole fading-to-black scene,
I was that glad.

Robert Hill Long

I'M A TEXAN NOW

Not long ago I moved to Texas,
and on a trip back home friends asked,
"Met any oil tycoons lately?
Gone on any cattle drives?"

"No," I said, "but last week at a party
I met a guy who knew a guy
who dated the sister of a Dallas Cowboys' cheerleader."
"Wow!" they said. "Wow!"

Gene Fehler

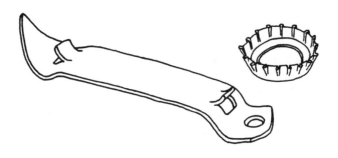

SOCIAL ZOOLOGY: PREP FOR A FIELD TRIP

In all the town of Malibu
You cannot find a caribou.
If you think you've spotted some on the loose,
Grazing the bar of the Malibu Ramada,
Wearing tams and with bellies as big as Jake LaMotta's,
Rub your eyes and look again:
They ain't caribou; they're Moose.

Gary Pittenger

SUBWAY SEASONING

On the final bleak day of February
a white-haired gent
in a red-striped jogging suit
and blue-and-white Nikes
opens his cardboard briefcase
extracts
a brown paper bag containing
a Diet Pepsi
swigs
and dips into the briefcase again
for a sand-colored napkin
dabs
and reaches in once more
for rainbow-bordered sun glasses
to ward off
the dazzlement of graffiti.

Eve Merriam

THE DAILY PLANET

"Because of a computer error, the Weather Records
and Forecasts printed in February incorrectly listed
the rising and setting times for Venus and Mars."
—*The New York Times*

O Martians, if you read the *Times*
(and this is just between us)
ignore the forecast, rise and set,
then pass the word to Venus!

Edward Watkins

THE ENCYCLOPEDIST'S CONUNDRUM

Whether it's
Skyscraper-sized hour glasses
Or the knee joints of hummingbird-sized sumo wrestlers:
I make line drawings and definitions of them at Plato's
       Warehouse of Forms.
A tiny Peruvian clepsydra,
The nose of a WWI aviator shot down over Romania:
These pose no problem.
But how do I measure the good time of an ant as he
Walks through a long macaroni elbow?

Kirby Olson

ENNUI

Not much happened today.
I saw a revolving fan
reflected in a spoon.

David Ray

APATHY

Jingley jangley
T. J. Fitikides
published a handbook of
Cypriot coins.

Numismatologists
chorus their cheers; but the

man in the street neither
listens nor joins.

IMITATION IS THE SINCEREST FLATTERY, BUT . . .

Dibbily daubily
G. A. Beltraffio
copied his master, ad-
hered to his style;

said Leonardo with
irascibility,
"Imitate somebody
else for a while!"

Blossom S. Kirschenbaum

MEMO TO MY MUSIC DEALER

Before the ocean-horns of symphony,
make fast my moorings now or I am drowned.
From buoys that bell and prelude sounds of sea,
from mermaids' moaning, keep me stopped and bound.
Please check: Tchaikowsky puts me in his power;
each cymbal-clash shanghais me from the shore;
with each boom-bum his kettle drums devour
like fuel all but this marinated core.
Oh, stall the vagrant Wagner's sailing-call:
his salty altos coo, his woodwinds greet
like gulls and woo me in a seaweed thrall.
I fear I'll try the tide in such mad heat
as surely must have sent, with wild alarms,
the Dutchman flying into Davy's arms!

A. L. Lazarus

CLOCKS AND LOCKS

Clocks and locks are fritzed, unsprung,
   the light bulbs sputter blue,
and round about the homefront fly
all manner of thing and thang and thung
   in rotational roundeloo.

This is the wisdom of no-reason-why
   in place of no-matter-how;
if everything clearly made clearly good sense
we'd figure a way to make sense give lie,
   at least if words would allow.

But no need to try, for the course of events
   leaves senseless the things we thought,
then newly balloons up clear bubbles to burst:
no one's reasoning mind prevents
   things being what they're not.

Ideas sound best I once thought worst,
   and much good taste turns bad,
and what's meant to stay still often stays
just long enough still to be seen reversed.
   And that which is had

is lost; that which is paid repays;
   tidiness leads to mess;
and it hits us closest which is farthest flung,
comes to us soonest that is put off for days:
   and certainty is always a guess.

Clocks and locks are fritzed, unsprung,
   the light bulbs sputter blue,

and round about the homefront fly
all manner of thing and thang and thung
   in rotational roundeloo.

Mark Rich

AMHERST NEIGHBORS

On lines from Emily Dickinson's letters

Do you recall old Mrs. Ay,
   with the nose of a hawk?
Last Monday-week she fledged
her antique wings and soared
   to her nest in Heaven.

Bee and Cee are closest comrades
   still. Together they walk,
   talk, eat—vote together!
They intend to be Jonathan
   and David, or Damon

and Pythias, or what's better,
   the United States of
   America! Mrs.
Dee grows larger, rolls down the lane
   to church like a marble.

I found Miss Ea in our garden
   peering at a purloined lily—
   bats think foxes have no
eyes. It comforts the criminal
   little to know the law

expires with him. Father feels ill—
    the straightest engine has
    its leaning hour. Madame
Gee goes tattling still. Her yard needs
    combing—no one can keep

a sumach and a secret too.
    And there is Aitch, of course—
    she looks a little tart,
but makes excellent pies after
    one gets acquainted. I

tend house and to a quiet hour.
    Miss Jaye grows so thin
    in her cottage of slats,
I could fancy that skeleton
    cats caught spectre

rats in dim old nooks and corners.
    Mr. Kaye is less lively
    than he was wont, if one might
discern it—there are those in the
    morgue that bewitch us with

sweetness, but that which is dead must
    go with the ground. To speak
    of wings yet again—sweet
Mrs. Elle comes with the robins.
    Robins have wings. Mrs.

Elle has wings. A society
for the prevention of wings would
be of benefit to us all.

Lewis Turco

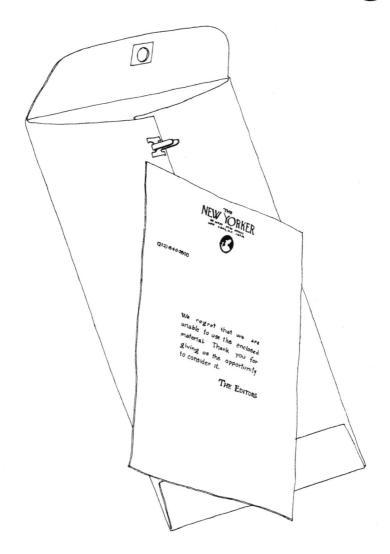

6

SHORT-TERM MEMORY LOSS

Toothpaste
Toilet paper
Towels

Those three spare lines
In my notebook. Now
I can't remember
Anything
About that poem.

But there they stand,
Three broken columns
Rising from the sand:

Toothpaste
Toilet paper
Towels

Tom Disch

MY LUCK

Wheres the fire he said and I said Officer
this terrific *ottava rima* has just hit me
and I simply must get to a typewriter
before I forget it and he said Lady
calm yourself whilst I write up your
ticket since any form that rhymes AB
ABABCC is by nature mnemonic
and in the future drive more eudaemonic

Bonnie Jacobson

"FOOL!" SAID MY MUSE TO ME:

Go to Surrey and Wyatt,
thou sluggard, or to Oldys,
Davies, Ralegh, Prior
and other Olden Goldies.

Read Fulke Greville, Landor,
Nashe, Greene, and George Chapman
(the poet, not the poisoner)———
and Dunbar, if you can.

Learn from Blake and Jonson,
Meredith, Smart, and Clough.
Stop posturing in blue jeans;
forget about that stuff

the TV ads call "life";
sit on your ass, and write!

G. N. Gabbard

PO BIZ

It's been a long time coming,
But after the Cavalier Poets
We've finally got the pedestrian ones,
Coming in on little flat feet.

Howard Nemerov

A SHORT POEM

Most poetry is of the longer sort
but I decided this one would be short.

James S. Koch

A PLAGUEY THING

If I were you I'd just forget it:
A pantoum is a plaguey thing.
It drives you crazy if you let it;
It haunts you, dawn and evening.

A pantoum is a plaguey thing.
My friend, can you define *pantoum*?
It haunts you, dawn and evening.
Does it belong in a drawing room?

My friend, can you define *pantoum*?
Do you strum it or pluck it or beat it?
Does it belong in a drawing room?
If fruit or veg, then you could eat it.

Do you strum it or pluck it or beat it?
Dare mail it to a little mag?
If fruit or veg, then you could eat it.
Producing it can be a drag.

Dare mail it to a little mag,
It drives you crazy if you let it.
Producing it can be a drag;
If I were you I'd just forget it.

Vonna Adrian

HAIKU

Seventeen sylla-
bles don't give you much time to
get oriented.

Edmund Conti

ON THE RHYMING OF FOUR-LINE VERSES

"In quatrains, single rhymes can serve,"
Euterpe said to Clio,
"But pairs of rhymes display more verve,
Panache, pizzazz, and brio."

J. F. O'Connor

ONE-UP

Swinburne found thirty-nine rhymes for Dolores
And I found another in my thesaurus.

Bruce Berger

UNPLEASANT SURPISE

I would have thouhgt
That ,
as stone as i am
, I wouldn"t be able to 2rite.

But that just isn¼t so .

Jay Dougherty

INSTEAD

Instead of writing this poem
this weekend,
I could have poisoned cabbage worms
in the garden, assassinated aphids
with a handy, multipurpose agent
invented by the Germans in World War II;
I could have attended the Democratic picnic,
barbecued my moustache
and played frisbee with the old farts;
I could have explained once again
to my neighbor that it's not the Kiwanis
itself—I'm sure they're a fine bunch
of leisure suits—I'm just not
a joiner; I could have strolled
downtown for the *New York Times*
in my bathrobe and slippers
not giving a good goddamn
what the churchgoers thought
and spent all Sunday reading it;
but instead, here I am again
wasting my time on you.

David Lunde

WRITING TO GET THROUGH THE NIGHT WHILE THE BABY CRIES

It doesn't matter that you're in there screaming.
I'm in here, toughening up my diction.
You're clean and dry and fed and the doctor said
you'd probably take a few days to learn
to sleep through the night. It's a good time
for me to learn to write nasty and flat,
no metaphor and lots of snide
foreign words for variety. Merde.
Your shriek rears up, silver as a palomino
in heat. That is, if palominos ever
rear up in heat. The only palomino
I ever saw was Trigger. She was a nice horse.
Not rude, like being in heat. Or children screaming.
She was the only friend Roy had, sometimes,
when things got mean. The way a child might be
the last good friend a person has.
Maybe Roy chose a palomino because
he thinks it means Pal Of Mine in Italian.
Palomino, there you go.
If only I knew a few more foreign words!
All right, Palomino, I'm coming.

Jeanne Murray Walker

THE CARE AND FEEDING OF A POET

is a noble task (whatever the
feminists may say) it insures

the caretaker a certain immor-
tality (if the poet is a good

one) and it also provides cer-
tain rewards in the here & now

such as typing manuscripts and
sending poems to magazines and

entertaining the wives of other
poets who come visiting (while

the geniuses sit in the study
drinking beer) and in certain

cases being informed that one
or more ancillary muses are re-

quired to provide inspiration.

James Laughlin

THE POET RIDICULED BY
HYSTERICAL ACADEMICS
—after the painting by DeLoss McGraw

Is it, then, your opinion
    Women are putty in your hands?
Is this the face to launch upon
    A thousand one night stands?

First, please, would you be so kind
    As to define your contributions
To modern verse, the Western mind
    And human institutions?

            Where, where is the long, flowing hair,
                The velvet suit, the broad bow tie;
            Where is the other-worldly air,
                Where the abstracted eye?

Describe the influence on your verse
    Of Oscar Mudwarp's mighty line,
The theories of Susan Schmersch
    Or the spondee's decline.

            You've labored to present us with
                This mouse-sized volume; shall this equal
            The epic glories of Joe Smith?
                He's just brought out a sequel.

            Where are the beard, the bongo drums,
                Tattered T-shirt and grubby sandals,
            As who, released from Iowa, comes
                To tell of wondrous scandals?

Have you subversive, out of date,
    Or controversial ideas?
And can you really pull your weight
    Among such minds as these?

            Ah, what avails the tenure race,
                Ah, what the Ph.D.,
            When all departments have a place
                For nincompoops like thee?

                                    W. D. Snodgrass

ENVOI

Ah, my poems, here you are—
you've come home again!
Here is that white envelope I folded,
hopeful as a spinster's linens,
the friendly black pica of my very own name typed by me,
my eager spittle under the sober head of each stamp.
My poems, who are so shame-faced as you greet me,
believe me I understand how you feel.
You've gone far and wide
from Chelsa, New York to Crete, Nebraska—
you have done your best
and nobody wanted you.

It's always the same:
the perfect vellum messages of sympathy from The Best
        Magazines,
the snippets of bright paper scrawled "Sorry"—
the teasers which start out "April 14 (I think!)"
Nobody wants you.
I can picture the scornful glances they gave you,
the heartless way they dismissed you (summarily, I'm
        sure),
the clips, spindles, staples with which they mauled you—
(Who do they think they are sticking pins in my images?)

What is this viscous smudge in the corner of a love
        poem—
a thumb print, Kraft mayonnaise, editor's ejaculant?
The odd little crease almost in the center of this ode—
Did some midget muezzin who is also a
graduate assistant in English at Morocco State
genuflect here, his hairpiece toward Mecca?
(Surely it is not fair to make fun of Moslems alone in this
        poem.

I will have to remember to include a Sister of Charity and
a Lubavitcher somehow later on.)

My poems, how I love you!
Do not feel rejected.
You must leave me again, but not for more than
6-8 weeks at most (slightly longer for *Partisan Review* or
recently defunct publications).
Let us sit awhile and have a few last drinks before you go.
I can't guarantee that I'll face another separation calmly,
    though.
I may follow you on my hard-working knees like the
    indomitable
Mothers of Russia, clinging to you with powerful biceps, my
babushka in glorious disarray, my peasant face buried in
    your
collective fly. (How come I always think of you as *men* by
    the way?)
My little spike heels will sink repeatedly into the desert
    sands
as I run after you in your trim Foreign Legion visors—
(How obliquely I am echoing an earlier reference here!)
Or perhaps I will turn, my clenched fists breaking
    through the
sleazy pocket linings of my old trench coat, my collar
    turned up
so that it keeps getting in the way of my Mexican
    earrings—
and simply walk away into the night.

My poems, my darlings,
I kiss you, I bless you, I pray that God (at least)
may keep you!

L. L. Zeiger

199 •

THE EDITOR REGRETS

When I consider how much time is spent
By people penning poems nationwide,
How talents under bushels yet must hide
As nought but flimsy printed slips are sent
To thank the poem's maker and present
The editors' regrets, but glad you tried . . .
"Do you expect subscriptions, print denied?"
I phone to ask. But editors resent
Veiled threats. This one replies: "Our journal needs
Neither your work, nor to be irked by test-
Y calls. (Get his mild joke?) I'll tell you straight:
Thousands without bidding send us screeds
From home *and* overseas. We print the best.
Until there's room your stuff can sit and wait."

David Cram

BLUE POEM

Roses are red,
  And poets are blue.
They wish they were roses,
  So they'd be read, too.

Hubert E. Hix

AT THE POETRY READING:
"THIS IS A POEM ABOUT THAT"

This will be my *last* poem tonight.
I want to share this experience with you.
When I read this poem, many people wonder

if this is a true story. Well,
it's true. This really happened.
This is dedicated to someone in this room.
Is this mike on?
There's a couple words in this poem you may not know:
formication: a spontaneous abnormal sensation of ants
or other insects running over the skin.
fubsy: somewhat fat and squat.
When I was at Iowa.
The 'I' in this poem isn't me.
The 'you' in this poem isn't me.
The you in this poem isn't the same you
as in the other poems.
At my last reading.
This is about a place I used to live
and people I used to know:
you don't know them.
My agent told me.
At dinner before the reading.
For this poem, I'll play my dulcimer
one octave lower.
I mailed this to my ex-wife
but got no response.
This is a famous unnamed writer in this poem.
When I was at Breadloaf.
Or was it Provincetown.
This is a long poem.
It's divided into sections.
When I run my hand through my hair
it's a new section.
We're negotiating movie rights.
I wrote this when I was depressed.
Please applaud.
Would you like to hear more?

Jim Daniels

THE LATIN AMERICAN SOLIDARITY COMMITTEE
FUNDRAISING PICNIC

"What we'd like to do," he said
"is include some local poets
in the entertainment."
"Sure," I said.
It was at the Mellon pavilion
in Frick Park and when I got there
they were running late. "Listen,"
he said, "I'm really sorry,
the poetry has to go later in the program
because we still haven't raffled off
the bottle of Cuban rum."
"Sure," I said,
After the Cuban rum there was an interlude
with mariachi music and solo guitar and
then a professor of sociology
gave a full account of his recent
trip to Cuba and how the Cuban people
despite having just broken the ubiquitous
chains of American economic exploitation
showed unfailing courtesy to visiting dignitaries
such as himself.
By this time it was almost dark.
"Jeez," he said, "if we have the poetry now
we'll never get in any volleyball."
"That's ok," I said, "I like volleyball."
So I played, and the other team was pretty good,
I got three balls spiked in my face.
After that I drank some beer and talked
with a pretty Mexican woman.
After the beer ran out I went home.
Under cover of darkness
the revolution was gathering steam.

Ed Ochester

A SLENDER BOOK OF VERSE
AND ITS PURCHASER

I praise, a rarity in these times,
This book of well-made rhymes,
And praise, whose rarity exceeds it,
One who buys and reads it.

F. C. Rosenberger

MY WIFE READS THE PAPER AT BREAKFAST
ON THE BIRTHDAY OF THE SCOTTISH POET

Poet Burns To Be Honored, the headline read.
She put it down. "They found you out," she said.

Miller Williams

THE RED-HANDLED HATCHET

dinner depends
upon

the red-handled
hatchet

wedged in the chopping
block

beside nervous
chickens.

Mark Sanders

SHAKESPEARE SONNETS CONVERTED INTO COUPLETS

152

(*The expense of spirit in a waste of shame*)
It's never good to give up all for lust—
and go all out to get it, tit or bust!

148

(*My mistress' eyes are nothing like the sun*)
She's not a goddess, spoiled by all that hype;
she isn't perfect, but she's still my type!

116

(*When to the sessions of sweet silent thought*)
Proustian remembrance makes old sorrows new—
but I feel better when I think of you!

8

(Shall I compare thee to a summer's day?)
Ah! Summer fades away, with some celerity,
but in my verse you'll live to charm posterity!

Gavin Ewart

DELIGHT IN ORDER, TOO

Her faded cutoffs shrunk tight and frayed,
Their sideseams split a few inches by full thighs,
Her hair in the breeze dangerously disarrayed,
At her sandy midriff the shirttails she loosely ties—
Say, "Let's get cozy now the ship's been wrecked."
No need for opening lines in the middle of the play.
The coconut milk mustache begs to be kissed away.
Sweet disorder's one look that's always correct.

But then, the lipstick, the stiletto heel,
The seamless mesh, the contoured silk confection
Whose plunges were dreamed with a scientific feel
For melting points, the cream of her complexion
Set off by a velvet neckband, saying, "Dare
To nestle here forever," the dance begun
By earrings at each bright glance—nature and art
Like stars' conjunction, precise in every part—
Are perfect, too. You're falling into the sun;
You're transparent. You can start anywhere.

Gary Selden

PAOLO'S VERSION

It ain't like we mean nobody no harm
Us sitting in the yard my brother's farm
But in this book is people doing stuff
You wonder how they stretch theirselves enough
I sees the thing I whizzes with is grown
Is what she reach her hands is grabbing on
I says what is you want we doing now
She says ain't no one never show you how
And I says no and she says it don't matter
Not knowing you don't is sometimes gets better
Then she is pull us lying in the grass
She shows me what and I does and she says
You sure you ain't done none this how you do
I says sure with the sheep but not like you
She says my god I thinks I going to swoon
I says it better be you do it soon
And there it is. All time this wind it blows
I hopes I finds her round and round she goes
You write this down if someone asking you
We has true love some five six minutes true.

Carl Judson Launius

BOOBIAT

Oh what a joy it is to see thee bow;
One furtive glance were paradise enow—
The vagrant hem, the hapless strap, and then
I shall behold a jug of thine, and wow!

Paul Humphrey

TO A FRINGED GENITAL

What was it? was Ruskin's foreskin stuck?
phimosis? or cryptical orchids? or a job
for Voronoff? Or the Victorian trick
of calling the human "bad taste"? Good taste was glab
or cast-iron-draped classic females in gardens,
heavy as "Mother" (tank, Mark I); the brunt

was left to men married at thirty discovering
hair. But self-abuse gainsays impotence
before and after marriage, and also during,
Ruskin admitted. What, then? if not some glad
obscure recognition of a beauty
not ever to be, not by him, disarrayed:
sex's shade snarled his forebrain, not fears,
closed his eyes, and pressed out angels' tears.

G. N. Gabbard

A LITERARY HISTORY OF CHEESE

Caedmon
Was thought a madman
For sharing with his geese
A whole petit-suisse.

John Bunyan,
Munching cheddar and onion,
Plotted his tale
In jail.

John Milton
Dined upon stilton
And mineral water
While dictating to his daughter.

John Dryden
Ate gouda from Leyden
Till turning R. C.,
Then converted to brie.

Robert Herrick,
Built like a barrack,
Said, "Blubber bedamn."
And gorged on edam.

George Herbert, the priest,
Ate no kind of beast,
But cottagers cheeses
While metering Jesus.

Alexander Pope
Would polish off a trope
Then turn with a hem
To boursin-triple-creme.

Alfred, Lord Tennyson
Would first give the benison
Then apply all his pressure
To slicing the cheshire.

Dante Rossetti
Preferred his spaghetti
Well laden with hits
Of Parmesan bits.

Oscar Wilde
Genially smiled
While being a punster
And reached for the muenster.

Robert Frost
Would inquire the cost
Before stopping his rick
And consuming some brick.

Roberta Simone

WHY CONTEMPORARY AMERICAN POETS RARELY WRITE EPIGRAMS OF THE QUALITY OF BEN JONSON'S "ON GUT"

Gut is still alive,
& he will lech, lust, & pander,
But Gut has a stable of lawyers
Who readily sue for slander.
Court costs & legal fees are such
No one criticizes Gut too much.

Louis Phillips

THE ROSE AND THE WORM

Willie Blake blasted the rose
Whose thorns had pricked his arm.
His sick rose died but deep inside
He found a healthy worm.

James Camp

A 4TH STANZA FOR DR. JOHNSON, DONALD HALL, & LOUIS PHILLIPS*

I put my hat upon my head
And walk'd into the Strand,
And there I met another man
Who's hat was in his hand.

The only trouble with the man
Whom I had met was that
As he walked swinging both his arms,
His head was in his hat.

Of course the head within the hat
Belonged to my friend Otis,
But I, since I am quite polite,
Pretended not to notice.

Yet as I strolled the hat-filled Strand
It struck me—strange to tell—
That every head was swinging loose
And so swung mine as well.

X. J. Kennedy

* 1st stanza by Samuel Johnson
2nd stanza by Donald Hall
3rd stanza by Louis Phillips

WITCHES' SABBATICAL

Swift is stern
and Sterne is swift;
social drag
exceeds our lift.

Sterne is swift
and Swift is stern;
fools may be learnèd,
but they never learn.

G. N. Gabbard

DUO FOR VOICE & PERCUSSION

We were discussing Alfred Noyes.
Howells said he'd never heard the sound
But added, "Once I heard Saul Bellow
I didn't mind hearing Ezra Pound."

E. O. Staley

A NOTE TOWARD A DEFINITION OF CULTURE

T. S. Eliot
Visiting the Orient
Found the hair of a dog in his hootch.
Said he, with disdain
To a dish of chow mein,
"Do I dare . . .
Do I dare eat a pooch?"

James Camp

GERTRUDE AND ALICE

Gertrude, that genius of her genus,
Explaining symbols such as 'phallus,'
Composed: "a pen is a pen is a penis . . ."
"Ah, that's the pen ultimate!" said Alice.

Joan Van Poznak

LITERARY RIVER RHYME

Standing by the River Ouse
Virginia got the wham wham blues;
Filled her pockets full of pebbles,
Stepped in. Glub, glub. End of troubles!

William Cole

BITTER GRAPES

I'd serve whatever time in hell
For a resonant name like Lawrence Durrell.
How could that most British churl
Choke it down to Lawrence Durrell?

Bruce Berger

ON SEEING GAVIN EWART IN SAINSBURY'S

It must be the Muse's day off,
And poets also eat.
So down from lofty heights into the street.

The shopping list: more grapes and pomegranates? Try
Finding nectar here on Putney High.
Can you imagine Swinburne
Emerging from The Pines
To purchase tins of beans
By Messrs Heinz?
Or Eliot . . . he dared to eat a peach,
But buy them? Fortnums, maybe,
Or on some Aegean beach.
Not on the Costa Putney
Where the natives quench their gluttony
To ritual choreography
In the brightly lit monotony
Of Sainsbury's.
Outside, the rhythm section of endless traffic furies,
Perfumes of a thousand and one lorries,
Inhabitants, pale and lumpy, rush and jostle,
Expressions blank, some friendly, some look hostile.
Do they know of greener grasses
Than this grey ground of the working classes?
And here's our local poet
Leaning on a wire trolley,
Perhaps it's just a decoy
While he observes the pageant of Man's Folly,
Stocks up on food for thought.
He watched it all.
I looked twice, caught his eye.
Was that returning glance a poet's,
Or mere curiosity?
I've read his dirty stuff . . .
My chicken and I hurried by,
Returned to cook the stew.
Did he go home and write a poem too?

Joan Van Poznak

WYSTAN HUGH AUDEN: A VILLANELLE

Why shun a nude tag?
Why stun a huge hand?
Hug a shady wet nun.

Why stand a huge Hun?
Why gash a dune nut?
Why shun a nude tag?

Guy hands u new hat,
Haw, the Sunday gun.
Hug a shady wet nun.

Why aghast, unnude?
Why a gash, untuned?
Why shun a nude tag?

Ashen guy dun what?
Why? Nag a shut nude.
Hug a shady wet nun.

Why daunt a snug he?
Why dun a gaunt she?
Why shun a nude tag?
Hug a shady wet nun.

David Lehman

FROM THE POETRY EXCHANGE, TWO CONVERSATIONS

1. Who is your favorite poet?
   This week it's George Herbert.
   Oh. Where does he teach?

2. Have you published any new poetry?
   My latest book came out two years ago.
   No, I meant *recently*.

Howard Nemerov

THE POET REDGROVE

> "Redgrove is one of the very few contemporary poets
> who actually blazes at his readers . . ."
>
> —a blurb

Quick! Hit the dirt! Take cover! Down!
The poet Redgrove's back in town

With weapons fiercer far than Byron's.
No man dare stand in his environs.

He's mad! He's mean! He's out to get you!
The undertaker's bound to fetch you

If you attempt to sneak one look.
For God's sake, reader! Drop that book!

Bruce Bennett

ON INSTANT LIVES

(*Howard Moss's Capsules
of Great Figures in the Arts*)

One feels that these
Biographees
Would read Howard Moss
With no sense of loss—
Except to wish they'd thought to be
Themselves with such economy.

Roy Blount Jr.

A SWITCHED CAREER

Clearer than limelight now, his future shone
True to the greased directions of his crayon:
Black ink astonishingly shimmered where it lay on
Luminous stone—

And in that gleam discovering lithography,
Alois Senefelder
Swallowed, and wiped the stone clean with his tragedy
Balder.

X. J. Kennedy

THE LAXNESS MONSTER;
or,
I BE SINGER;
or,
SAUL BELLOW, WELL MET;
or,
INEXPLICABLE SPENDING ON IONIAN WHITES AND GOLDINGS

You're
An obscure
Slav
Nobody ever heard of?

The Paul Anka
Of Sri Lanka
The torpors of whose serendipitous pantoums equal
Those of *The Odyssey: A Modern Sequel?*

The Olivia
De Havilland of Bolivia
Locally notorious for turgid verse
Worse
Even than that of whoever it was was a.k.a. Saint-John
    Perse?

Talk mysterious?
Take yourself too serious?
Relax. Don't you realize
You're probably next in line for the Nobel Prize?

What lies East of Eden?
Sweden.

William Harmon

THE DEATH OF THE REFERENCE LIBRARIAN

From my mother's sleep I fell into the stacks;
I ate cream cheese and jelly and wiped my nose.
Six years later, loosed from my dream of life,
I woke to find myself paginated, numerical.
When I died they bound me and added me to the rows.

David Kirby

KNOPF AND DUTTON

Knopf is Knopf and Dutton is Dutton;
Dutton's not Knopf, and Knopf isn't Dutton.
Dutton means nothing,
and Knopf means a button.

Gavin Ewart

PIÈCE DE RÉSISTANCE

A book of Metaphysics
is an artichoke to me:
on every page
to whet the sense
a smidge of succulence
(diminishing, it's true,
as one leafs through).
But ah, the transcendental smack—
the gourmet knows it!—
when once you read the last page back
and close it.

Ann Deagon

PROOFREADER'S ISLAND

Afraid he's about
To lose his mind,
That another typo
Will drive him blind,

He decides to give
His skipper the slip,
And dives from the rail
Of the editorship.

Reaching the beach,
His happiness grows—
He hears the cawing
Of the pilcrows.   ¶

On the shore his son,
Blonded and tanned,
Builds a castle
In the ampersand.   &

His daughter, playing
With her rabbit,
Lets it nibble
On a caret.   ∧

But soon the press gang
Will cross the waves
To re-shanghai
Their galley slave.

Michael Spence

SYNTAX

Here the hero. . . , having failed satisfactorily to resolder the broken sword, wakes . . . in a flowery meadow.

—Jessie L. Weston, *From Ritual to Romance*, 1920

And when she
had suc-
ceeded unsatis-
factorily
in passing sentence,
she graced the hero with
a state of nature
so rare
these latter days
it draws me back
to prayer,
long years forsaken:
Oh
may my failure be
satisfactory
and may I too awaken
thus in a flowery meadow.

Robert Canzoneri

HOLE

One-letter alphabet,
it writes itself
in the circle O.
Golfers go for it;
gophers run for it.
Most folks don't need one
in their heads; others

have them already.
It's breezy, hollow
as a caroler's note,
a puff of smoke.
Poles fit in, rubber
rolls around, and
lids slide over.
It trips a foot,
tempts a poke.
Fingers form it 'ok.'
It's a place to blow,
to darn, to sit,
with a sound-alike
meaning quite the opposite.

Imogene Bolls

AN APOTHEGM

is a proverb
that hasn't caught on yet.

Like this one.

Daniel Hoffman

EMPHASIS MINE

When reading a slam
Of another's views
I don't give a *damn*
Whose italics are whose.

Edmund Conti

PATIENT

My reading program has increased;
No longer is it scanty.
I'm catching up on all the greats
Like Dickens, Twain, and Dante.

The program is a simple one.
I do not need a proctor.
I simply take a book to read
While waiting for the doctor.

Keith Baker

"THESE STUDENTS COULDN'T WRITE THEIR WAY OUT OF A PAPER BAG"

—Anonymous

I gather groups of freshmen. I distribute
blue books and pens, then unveil the bag
big as a bus.

They rush in and I twist the opening.
There is much classified argot, many
contempo shibboleths but, sure enough,
nobody is writing his way out.

Still, the bag is moving rhythmically.
There are unified, coherent and adequately
developed moans. Whatever they are doing
has a beginning, middle and end.

"I want to give you all A's," I shout
as the bag develops an afterglow and
damp spots appear all over the place.

Ron Koertge

JESSA'S LATE ASSIGNMENT

She hides out in Creative
Writing II,
her biology notebook spread

like the scattered yellow
leaves in a wind storm.
I read to her the title of a poem,

"Estrella En El Pozo,"
she glances up
from her *prunus virginiana*

and translates
"Stars in the Night."
I tell her no, "Stars

in the Hole." She says nothing,
pastes another label
and writes in parenthesis

the common chokecherry.

Al Ortolani

GREAT PLAINS LIT

Students don't like Wright Morris.
They say, "His books bore us."
And I know they'd rather
not read Willa Cather.

Mark Sanders

IN MEMORY OF AN ENGLISH PROFESSOR

Our dear soul
Might have lived longer if someone had sent it away
On somebody's yacht,
Telling it gently not to let anything fray
Its nerves, no matter what.
But since of all possible luxuries most it deplored
Getting packed,
It decided to stay on the job and be cured
Or cracked.

The trouble was that Harry of Hapless Hall
Sat in its class at the back,
And Harry, yare yokel, pride of the breed, was a yak
Who like a yak bore
The burden of Lycidas, Lucy, Endymion, Lucy, Lucy and
        Ganymede
With ever increasing yakor,

Until yak and the spirit of yak
Triumphed over that class both in front and in back,
And our dear soul, not Harry, broke.

Reed Whittemore

7

THE NEW REGIME

Yes, I agree. We'll pull ourselves together.
We eat too much. We're always getting pissed.
It's not a bad idea to find out whether
We like each other sober. Let's resist.
I've got the Perrier and the carrot grater,
I'll look on a Scotch or a pudding as a crime.
We all have to be sensible sooner or later
But don't let's be sensible all the time.

No more thinking about a second bottle
And saying 'What the hell?' and giving in.
Tomorrow I'll be jogging at full throttle
To make myself successful, rich and thin.
A healthy life's a great rejuvenator
But, God, it's going to be an uphill climb.
We all have to be sensible sooner or later
But don't let's be sensible all the time.

The conversation won't be half as trivial—
You'll hold forth on the issues of the day—
And, when our evenings aren't quite so convivial,
You'll start remembering the things I say.
Oh, see if you can catch the eye of the waiter
And order me a double vodka and lime.
We all have to be sensible sooner or later
But I refuse to be sensible all the time.

Wendy Cope

TWO HOORAYS FOR HOLIDAYS

On holidays, like weekends,
You'll never see me frown:
I don't get up to go to work,
And my stocks do not go down!

Ned Pastor

WE AND THE WEEKEND

When do we say we'll do it,
Paint it, repair it, or glue it,
Write it, or wax it, shampoo it?
　　Over the weekend's the phrase.
Then, do we get to mend it,
Dye it, re-cane it, or tend it,
Solder it, polish it, send it?
　　A weekend is only two days!
"Over the weekend," we say,
To chores that confront us today,
Invoking a modest delay.
　　That's when the wheels will revolve!
Do they? We'd like to say Yes.
But sheepishly we must confess:
A weekend is no more or less
　　Than a weak end to highest resolve!

Alma Denny

AGAINST WAKING EARLY

I'd like to knock
my body's clock

clean off some shelf
inside myself!

A BIT OF ENLIGHTENMENT

You open your eyes one morning
and find yourself
not in bed.
Your clothes are on,
your hair is combed,
your belly's full,
your teeth are brushed,
you seem to have survived once more
your morning sojourn on the bus.
You're at work, dummy,
without any of the in-betweens.
But are you grateful?
"Hey, what's going on here?"
you say.
There's no pleasing some people.

Tom Riley

BUSINESS LUNCHEON

I open cans for lunch—
"Seafood Feast" for the cat,
"Chicken of the Sea" for me.
It occurs that we may be eating
Separate parts
Of the same fish . . .
(I am *told* they are separate parts).

At first we are disgusted,
Then we understand:
It has always been this way,
And this is what we do
For a living.

Joel Ferree

THE FAIR FOWL

News item: Mayo Clinic endorses chicken soup as
treatment for the common cold.

Among the prescriptions
Of ancient Egyptians
An essence of chicken was held in esteem.
The Chinese had oodles
Of needles and noodles,
And using their noodles, made chicken supreme.

In subsequent ages,
Wise sages wrote pages
On sipping the soup that suppressed every wheeze.
In hovel and castle,
The prince and his vassal
Used extract of chicken to cure all disease.

Now cautious assessing
Has given its blessing
To primitive balm with a modern allure.
The Mayas extolled it;
The Mayos uphold it:
The soup of the coop is assurance of cure.

Robert N. Feinstein

E PLURIBUS OVUM

> "Our L'Eggs fit your legs"—pantyhose ad.

Your "*L'Eggs*" make (or makes) not a particle
Of sense, is a Frenchman's rebuff:
"*Les*" is the genuine article—
Or, better, *un oeuf* is enough.

Bob McKenty

PEJORATIVE

It's
   Mit der Dummheit
worse
than a
   Kaempfen Götter
crime,
it's a
   *Selbst Vergebens**
blunder.

Ernest Kroll

* "Against stupidity even the gods struggle in vain."

THE COURT RESTS

> News item: Mistrial declared in German court when a
> magistrate is found asleep.

While a witness is deposing, such a sin as quiet dozing
   Is forbidden;
Though the arguments be boring, the most delicate of
   snoring
   Can't be hidden.

So the verdict, when decided, though it may have been
    misguided
    As recorded,
Not to plaintiff nor defendant, but to Morpheus
    ascendant,
    Was awarded.

                         Robert N. Feinstein

P$$$$$T

O, espionage looked starry in the days of Mata Hari
But it's fallen to a sorry state indeed:
The glamour and the swagger of the old-time cloak and
    dagger
Is too high-class for the current spy-class breed.

Daily headlines are announcing that the FBI is pouncing
Upon spies who're wholly lacking in panache
And the glimpses we're afforded make their motivations
    sordid:
They're simply into spying for the cash.

As more dissident defectors go to work as spy detectors,
We can see so wild a paper-passing spree
That the evidence is striking, though perhaps not to our
    liking:
Espionage is now a cottage industry.

                         Felicia Lamport

DISCOUNT STORE

The wares are bright and cheap as a one-line poem.

G. N. Gabbard

BINGOHOLIC

She's not addicted. Oh, no!
She'll play till she wins and then go.

Shirley Vogler Meister

CURRICULUM CHANGE

My son's not keen on Music,
And Chemistry's too tough;
Physics is for bookworms,
Of Lit he's had enough.
Philosophy is boring,
Math drives him up the wall;
I hope he nets a million—
He's now pro-basketball!

Ned Pastor

ON A COMPLIMENT

You said I was perceptive, had a mind of quality.
But you're not very perceptive, so I'm bothered.

R. P. Dickey

ESKIMO HAIKU

Drip. Drip. Drip.
Spring has come to my living room!

Robert Peters

THREE

Henny Youngman Haiku

My father, the drunk,
saw ad, "Drink Canada Dry."
So he went up there.

Joan Rivers Haiku

Married so many times,
Heidi Abromowitz has
rice scars on her face.

Rodney Dangerfield Haiku

My wife can not cook.
Flies commit suicide at
our house—no respect.

Charles West

CROSS WORDS

Across and down
Till my head is reeling,
I'm filled in
On your every feeling.

Edmund Conti

DIAL-A-SHRINK

News item: Shrink Link, a telephone counseling service for executives, is now available to the general public. For a fee of $19 for every ten minutes you stay on the line, a psychiatrist will listen to your problem and offer some advice or suggestions. Payment must be made with a credit card.

Oh, how lucky, harried brethren!
What an unexpected find!
You can dial-a-shrink for counsel
And regain your peace of mind.

Is your marriage turning sour?
Can't you take its bumps and curves?
Dial-a-shrink for 19 smackers—
Let him calm your frazzled nerves.

Does the office grind disturb you?
Are its pressures too severe?
Take a shrink-break, soothe your psyche,
Watch your anguish disappear.

But regardless of your problem,
Just be sure to keep it brief;
If you gab as long as I do,
Next you'll need some debt relief!

Ned Pastor

NOT WHAT WE HAD IN MIND

Events can whittle us
Down to size
So we don't feel wise
But otherwise.

May Richstone

OLD WOMEN ARE TAKING OVER THE WORLD

Look at yourself,
reader: you are
young. And minute by
minute Old Women are
Taking Over the World.
You are reading.
Why in the hell
are you reading?
I know: you are reading
because there are a hundred
other things you should be doing,
none of which you want to.
Reading allows you to
goof off in the name of Ed
ification. This piece, I'm
afraid, is meant to stir you
into action. Action! Action!
Just like in the days of
Paul Revere. Old Women are
Taking Over The World!
Turn the page!

Jay Dougherty

VITA LONGA, CARS BREVIS

The varnished dashboard long ago was chipped,
The tarnished mascot wobbles in the wind,
The leather seats irreparably cracked,
The sports saloon slides slowly to its end,

Driven by a smelly, surly youth
Whose cigarette is dangling from his mouth.
Rainfall leaks in through the sunshine roof.
Need approachng death be so uncouth?

The wireless a tactless new accretion,
Blaring raucous sounds of roll and rock,
Could not the youth have exercised discretion
Before he plonked that liquid diode clock
On the dashboard with veneereal disease?

As to the sunstrip, may I ask you please
Avert your eyes; predictably inane,
It implies that Kevin loves Elaine.

Mark Stocker

OH, DEM OLDEN SLIPPERS!

No matter they are down-at-heel,
Thin-at-sole, demolished, beat,
So long as they still come between
The stone cold floor and my feet;
No matter they are shapeless, torn,
Tacky, tattered, long outworn . . .
I glide into them gratefully
As a *bateau* to its *quai*.
I vow that someone else, not I,
Will have to throw them away.
And I'm bequeathing Grade A bonds
To anyone who'll have them bronzed.

Alma Denny

OLDER IS SAFER

When I was one, in a single year
I doubled my age, so why should I fear
And overreact to the passage of time—
It'll take dozens of years to double where I'm.

Robert N. Feinstein

AT SEVENTY

Each morning I scan the obituary page
And take comfort from the corpse's age.
If younger, I have beaten this I know.
If older, I still have years to go.

F. C. Rosenberger

THE GIRL NEXT DOOR

The girl next door was circumspect and neat.
She looked both ways to step across a street.

You'd scarcely think a truck would run her down
and kill her in an open dressing gown.

Yet there she lies, and surely she is dead.
A wheel has scraped the pavement with her head.

The neighbors have arrived and will agree
that it's an unexpected thing to see.

Some turn their eyes away, but others stare.
There's not a button fastened anywhere.

Her mother's hanging wash up in the cellar.
Someone should go down there at once and tell her.

But no one wants to face her with a fact
requiring sympathy as well as tact.

Knute Skinner

ELEGIES IN A CITY CHURCHYARD

Dentist

No use has he
For probes and drills—
This cavity
He amply fills.

Dowager

Many weep
At knowing she
Has to keep
Low company.

Decorator

Apartment black,
Of earthen floor,
And utter lack
Of chic décor.

Stripper

When Death gets dull
And disregards,
She winks her skull
And shakes her shards.

Gloria A. Maxson

POMPOUS

Pompous is dead. Put him to rest in style.
This protocol must last him for a while.

Paul Ramsey

ON A DECEASED OFFICE-SEEKER

At last elected this low place to fill,
No longer running now, but lying still.

Laurence Perrine

ON A LATE SCHOOLBOY

Now dead but never quick, he lagged to school,
Made smart no wise by wit but just by rule;
Now taught at length, and gravely, to persever,
He'll not be late again to school forever.

Laurence Perrine

ON A REFORMED SINNER

He's given up his wickedness for good.*

Laurence Perrine

* Claimed by its author to be the shortest blank verse poem in the language.

SMOKER'S EPITAPH

There isn't much that's left to tell.
Her life was a brief inhale and farewell.

John D. Engle, Jr.

EPITAPH FOR THE LEMON LADY

I sold good fruit;
Time squeezed me dry.
My rind lies here.
I'm in the sky.

Bruce Bennett

EPITAPH

She never developed the talents
With which Nature had endowed her.
She thought opportunity would knock
A little louder.

Lois Leurgans

AMADEUS

The day we opened Mozart's coffin
We found him sitting up and often
With huge eraser rubbing at a
Copy of an old cantata.

"What are you doing, Amadeus?"
We cried together. "You dismay us—
Erasing when you should be dozing!"
He answered, "Boys, I'm decomposing!"

LoVerne Brown

WHAT DID THE MIDGE SAY TO THE MILDEW?

You mold the rose,
I'll gall the copse.

Bonnie Jacobson

MRS. WILSON, WHO NEVER LOVED

Mrs. Wilson, who never loved
    my dog,
Has really learned to hold her tongue,
    by God,
    cause Dog
Tore up her flowers and
    she said,
    "My Fred
Will simply have a stroke!"
    And he did.
    And he's dead.

Virginia Long

MOWER AND MOWER

My neighbor bought a newer mower,
but seldom uses it. I guess
he likes his older mower more
or likes his newer mower less.

John D. Engle, Jr.

HOME OWNER'S LAMENT

A workday is from sun to sun;
A weekend's work is never done.

Pier Munn

MY LAWN IS BROWN AND ALL MY NEIGHBORS ARE PAINTING THEIR HOUSES AGAIN

Falling into the cracks between the black
and white piano keys isn't easy.
You have to spend at least
four hours every day never practicing.
And if you ever miss
even one day,
if only once you weaken
and give in to temptation
and absent-mindedly plink out the simplest
of melodies with your index fingers,
then you will never be as bad
a pianist as you could have been,
and people who hate music will know
that you've been practicing on the sly.

Tom Hansen

SEEDAM

It's evergreen, it blooms in spring;
Its proper name is Seedam.
You plant these plants between your flowers
So you don't have to weed 'em.

Lily D. Angle

A HEX FOR MY NEIGHBOR'S GREEN THUMB

May your shovel break, may your fertilizer bake,
May your droughts be long and dusty.
May moles make holes, may blights take tolls,
May your pruning tools get rusty.

A killing frost on the hybrids you crossed,
May your pink chrysanthemums sicken.
A pox on your phlox, may your seeds fall on rocks,
May your aphids and mealy-bugs thicken.
And to add to your woes, may you slice up your hose
When you run your power mower.
One last incantation: While you're on vacation
May stinkweed grow up to your door.
At the next Garden Show they'll surely know
Just who should have gotten first prize.
My brow with sweat was twice as wet,
And twice as green were my eyes!

Glenna Holloway

THE COST OF A STING

In build, the worker bee is weak:
To sting you strips him of his beak
And takes his teeth and lower lip off.
Which serves him right. But what a rip-off.

X. J. Kennedy

READING OUTDOORS

Gnat, have you landed here to look
for friends within my open book?
Though they are black and feeler-thin
these letters are no insect kin.
But if I slammed it shut you'd be
their brother in typography.

Joan Drew Ritchings

INSECTS BLIND TO HISTORY

The flea that bit Caesar's ass when he sat
In the Senate, was not one who cared to be a part
Of history. He was simply a part of the food chain,
Like it or not (he did) and though it is recorded
By Catullus or Seneca that Caesar often had spasms,
It was not true. He was part of the food chain, his
Skin was a tenderloin steak, and he couldn't get the
Fleas out of his toga, although he could drive the
Scots up into the moors, and push the Gauls into
Germany.

My own war with the fleas is going
Better, though I admit I'm wounded.
If I was his strategic advisor,
I'd have told him to put pans filled with water
Around his living room. Put a
Slow candle in the center of each pan.
The fleas jump
Towards the heat of the candle's flame,
Land in the moat,
          and perish.
In two hours it is possible to get twenty fleas
To go for this trick.
Caesar might have awarded me a generalship.
It is not necessary to move the pans around or disguise
      them.
Insects are blind to history.

Kirby Olson

PORCUPINE SONNET

Picking up drops from under one of my apples,
I see by a farther tree I claim as mine
A small fur hat some passing Russian's left.
It moves. Black eyes, stub tail: the porcupine.

He surrounds an apple, mouths his way around it,
And waddles off to find a sixteenth course.
Although he'd like to, he doesn't eat enough
To force me into any display of force.

Two nations not at war and not at peace,
We treat each other with benign neglect,
Gnawing in silence, silently filling boxes—
A tolerant coexistence I suspect

Sooner or later I'll have somehow to pay for,
And make him pay for.

Charles W. Pratt

I HYPNOTIZE BUGS

I hypnotize bugs
Into believing
They are world leaders.
I put them together
In a Mason jar.
So far there has been
A frank exchange
Of ideas.

Eugene A. Craig

HIDING PLACE

A speaker at a meeting of the New York State Frozen
Food Locker Association declared that the best hiding
place in event of an atomic explosion is a frozen-food
locker, where "radiation will not penetrate."

—News item

Move over, ham
   And quartered cow,
My Geiger says
   The time is now.

Yes, now I lay me
   Down to sleep,
And if I die,
   At least I'll keep.

Richard Armour

FABLE OF THE TERRORIST MOUSE

"No Mouse is an Iland
Unto Himselfe,"
Mused a murderous mouse
On a kitchen shelfe;

"When Louie died
Behind the wall,
They had to fumigate
The Hall;

Raskolnikoff
Who had the plague
In Singapore
Purged half of Prague;

"The pregnant Duchess
Of Dijon
Met Pierre on the stair—
Boeuf bourguignan!

"And I
Have merely arched my back
And caused a serious
Heart attack!"

He stamped his foot
To send a small
Vibration
To the Taj Mahal,

And wandered off
All by himself
Down the empty plain
Of the kitchen shelf.

Scott Bates

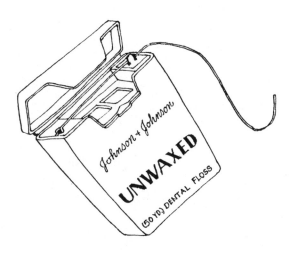

EIGHTH AND BROAD

In the warming sun the dog sleeps through the morning.
Primroses open at the curb,
Sparkle the dew and broken glass.
The old lady in a wig walks her pocketbook.
The grocer changes his sign.
The happy hangover walks a cigarette,
Hands free to paddle the air,
Snap his fingers and jive. The line
Starts outside community blood and plasma.
The Southern blows at 10th Street.
Rock shrimp, conch, crab legs,
Turkey wings, streak-o-lean.
We accept food stamps.
The law's in the cruiser
Lifting watermelon from Food World.

Wallace Whatley

BESIDES

As he handed over the wallet,
he felt the knife withdraw

from his throat. He thought of yelling,
but the only policeman he saw

was kissing a girl in the shade.
Besides, he still had more respect

for passion than for violence.

Mark Irwin

THE FRIENDS OF THE FRIENDS

he will flip the brittle disc
no a pizza no the gentle fruit
of the Frisbee Pie Company of
New Haven, Connecticut   no the
hubcap no the diaphragm *really*
the least lens   friend will thee
not make up thee's mind
he will put the disc
the oyster slide-on-Spode
no the parasol (*absit* handle)
the pepperonis of said pizza
under the mercy the lid at a clip
friend I would not hurt thee for the world
but thee stands where I am about to shoot

Caroline Knox

THE CITY MOUSE AND THE COUNTRY MOUSE

I have been thinking of being a guru
               or maybe a thinker
said the city mouse to the country mouse
and that is why I am standing here with my baggage
in your pleasant *merde* in the meadow
                    where is my suite?

I have no sweet
said the country mouse
not even a *tarte aux cerises*
               or a *bombe glacée*
                    or a *mousse aux framboises*

251 •

and I think you must be some sort of a nut to leave the
          bright lights
     I yearn for the bright lights
I would willingly give up all the *merde* in the meadow
          by golly
     for the bright lights

well said the city mouse
     you may take the bright lights
I'll take a hill in the sun in the *merde* in the meadow
     for the bright lights
a hill in the *merde* to sit on and fold my hands on
     for the bright lights

it's a free country
said the country mouse
and left for the city
where he had *mousse d'orange à l'ananas*
               and *gateau aux noix*
                    and *chantilly meringuée*

while the city mouse
sat on his hill in the *merde* in the meadow
interlocking his fingers
he had always wondered what should be done with the
          fingers
should he fold them?
               with palms on the paunch?
should he construct an inverted v?
               with the fingertips slightly touching?

so here I am back said the country mouse cheerily
          slapping
the city mouse on the back in the *merde* in the meadow
     I bring you

greetings from all those loose easy mice in the city
which is a nice place to visit
                by golly
though I wouldn't want to live there
                by golly
though I may go back Friday
for some of their *pithiviers*
                and *mille feuilles à la fondue*
                        and more *mousse aux*
                                        framboises

dear cousin country mouse
said the city mouse
you are surely a fast mouse
having already lived high on the *mousse* in the big city
returned from the big city
and made plans to go back again to the big city
                on Friday
while here I am sitting here in the *merde* as you left me
having not had my supper yet
it isn't easy
        being a guru
on this hill
                in the pleasant *merde*
                                in the meadow

                                Reed Whittemore

HAND

Pinky wiggled, "End, begin—
in is out, out is in."
Middle finger swaggered, "Oh,
I'm the highest skin can go."
Index finger wagged, "Ahem,
I direct the rest of them."
Thumb shrugged, "I can rub among
four fingers like a harlot's tongue."
Finger-next-to-pinky laughed,
"Bone's the pivot, bone is daft."

Mark McCloskey

EGO AT THE WHEEL

The loner off
   with his "I am!"
gets hemmed in by
   a loner jam

and looks about
   his budgeless car
and will not grudge
   how much "We are!"

Ernest Kroll

THE BOY WHO KILLED HIS MOTHER

In a dear little vine covered cottage
   On Forty-second Street
A butcher once did live who dealt
   In steak and other meat

His son was very nervous
    And his mother him did vex
And she failed to make allowance
    For his matricide complex

    And now in old Sing Sing
    You can hear that poor lad sing

Just a boy that killed his mother
    I was always up to tricks
When she taunted me I shot her
    Through her chronic appen*dix*
I was always very nervous
    And it really isn't fair

I bumped off my mother but never no other
    Will you let me die in the chair?

II

He was only sixteen and a fraction
    A' had ne'er been ail in his life
He had scarcely been fired from his high school
    For raping the principal's wife

Now he sits in the law's foulest dungeons
    Instead of his families embrace
Oh how would you like it your ownself
    If you stared the hot seat in the face

    So write Franklin D. if you can
    To send him to old Mattewan

Just a boy that killed his mother
    Now he's in a sorry fix

Since he up one day and plugged her
　　Through her perfect thirty-six
It was no concern of no one's
　　And his trial wasn't fair

The fact that he shot her was a family matter
　　Will you let him die in the chair?

III

Do you think that our civilization
　　Should punish an innocent lad
Why he said to the judge in the court room
　　He was aiming the gun at his dad

But the judges denied his petition
　　And at dawn on the 9th of July
Unless Governor Roosevelt shows kindness
　　Gus Schnlitski must certainly die

　　And the death house once again
　　Does ring to this refrain

Just a boy that killed his mother
　　With a brace of stolen colts
On *July* 9 they'll fill me
　　With a hundred thousand volts
It was dope that made me do it
　　Otherwise I wouldn't dare

'Twas ten grains of morphine that made me an orphine
　　Will you let me die in the chair?

F. Scott Fitzgerald

VIET KONG

Each one showed me his gold medal,
talismans from F-b-i, a name too holy
for them to say. These agents wished
to trade questions for answers, something like
the cult of "Jeopardy." "Why do you spell it
with a 'K'?" they asked. I told them I knew
the state capitals but I did not know
spelling. I asked if I could try another
category, perhaps state capitals.
They said they believed I was being smart,
which is taboo, that I could remain silent.
I take this Fbi to be a jealous god,
full of paradoxes and taboos, but perhaps
not so good on state capitals.

William Trowbridge

MRS. WHITEHOUSE'S VIEW OF
SEXUAL INTERCOURSE*

Well, he stuck his What Cannot Be Mentioned
into *her* What Cannot Be Mentioned
and they began to move a bit—
then they both went into a kind of epileptic fit
culminating in an explosion.
And that was more or less it.

Gavin Ewart

---

* Mrs. Whitehouse is a Censor of other people's morals, very willing to condemn indecency in plays, films and TV programmes that she herself has not seen.

[*SIC*] TRANSCRIPT GLORIA, *or*
THE BODY POLITICIAN

The transcript records that day's dark admonition
(the tape turning from reel ominous to real grim):
Ehrlichman's cold voice, but Colson's errant vision
of Dean—"He says you got an *ass* on your bosom."
We have been left to picture the infernal scene.
Here a weasel's, there a wolfish, or woeful, grin
gleams, then all leers dim: the crook of a question mark
is dully chiseling its stigma on the boss's brow
—beneath which one drab eye from its dank crevice now
scuttles, and gapes for light in the nightmare murk.
(The tape skips a beat, then loses heart altogether.)
But, his accusing finger, his stage hiss at once
apocalyptic, confidential, some damned dunce
sagely explicates: "A burro on your breast, sir"
—whose deeper frown demands higher truth, plainer wit.
"Oh, Mr. President—there's a mule on your tit!"

Irving Feldman

THE EXAMINER'S DEATH

Her life was blameless, blameless—
so when the Drivers' License Examiner died
she went straight to the Vestibule of Heaven.
It was crowded but after two centuries
she reached the desk. "Take a number,"
said St. Christopher. "We'll call you."

"Two centuries, and you'll call me?" she said.

"You should've made an appointment," the saint
    mumbled,
rubbing his halo like a hubcap.

"How do you do that?"

"Not my department," he said. "Take a seat."

The Drivers' License Examiner could hear
choirs singing and the still hum of suns
buzzing like mopeds through the empyrean.
This is timelessness, she thought. *There is
no time.* Shadows pooled and diminished,
pooled and diminished; forests rose and tumbled
beneath sheets of ice. In her dreams
her husband laughed his little
cough of a laugh.

When her number was called
the man at the desk looked like God,
his eyes dark as inkpads.

"Do you have your Death Certificate?" he asked.

"How could I? I was dead when they issued it!"

"Keep your voice down," said God, pursing his lips.
"We've got a problem."

Peter Meinke

EARLENE SPRATT'S LOT

Except for the half dozen Sam Pyle rents out behind his
    store,
Earlene Spratt owns the only mobile home in town.
It's pink, got a few bullet holes,

and looks like the next thunder gust might sink it.
Earlene knows people'd like to burn it down.
So last Saturday morning in the post office,
after Earlene asks how come she only gets mail
from Sears, Ames, and the Dollar Store,
and the postmistress bends over the counter
like she might split, but smiles and says,
"You don't get mail because your friends can't write,"
Ray Dillard walks in and says, "I hear you're leaving
town, Earlene. Moving to Maryland with your boyfriend."
Earlene says, "No. Daryl's buying me a new trailer
        instead:
a fifty-five foot mobile home, twelve foot wide."

Everybody in the post office (it's just a shed
off the postmistress's kitchen) is listening hard
and tells Earlene she can't put another trailer in.
It's against the building code.
You have to build or keep the one you've got.
Besides, you can't drag the trailer over Nelson
Wood's privet hedge. You can't cut those hedge apples
Larry Nichols planted along your back line.
And Daryl's two shade trees block the front. Earlene,
you're boxed in pretty good.

Earlene found herself a hillbilly with a crane.
He worked from the road, lifted both homes over Daryl's
shade trees, and set the new one tight between Nelson
        Wood's
privet hedge and Earl Skinner's
chain link fence. Earlene's got a fifty-five foot
mobile home on a fifty-five foot lot.

Hilary Russell

ACKNOWLEDGMENTS

All poems not listed hereunder are printed for the first time in *Light Year '87*; copyright remains vested in the poets. The following poems, previously copyrighted, are reprinted by permission of their authors or as otherwise indicated.

Richard Armour. "Money," "The Conscience," "To Have and Too Old," "Sequence," and "Hiding Place": © by Richard Armour.

Keith Baker. "Patient": © 1981 by Keith Baker. First appeared in *The Wall Street Journal*.

Dick Barnes. "Helendale": © 1976 by Dick Barnes. First appeared in *The Beloit Poetry Journal*.

Scott Bates. "Guide to Paris: Eiffel Tower, Versailles": © by Scott Bates. First appeared in *The Southern Poetry Review*.

James Camp. "From an Athlete Living Old," "The Race," "The Rose and the Worm," and "A Note Toward a Definition of Culture": © 1984 by James Camp. First appeared in *Cincinnati Poetry Review*.

William Cole. "What a Friend We Have in Cheeses!": © 1972 by William Cole. Reprinted from *And Be Merry*.

Wendy Cope. "The New Regime": © 1986 by Wendy Cope. First appeared in *The Observer* (U.K.).

David Cram. "Tunnel Vision": © 1986 by David Cram. First appeared in *The Sunday Times* (U.K.).

Barbara Crooker. "Field Guide to North American Birds": © 1985 by Barbara Crooker. First appeared in *The Beloit Poetry Journal*.

William Virgil Davis. "I-35, South of Waco": © 1979 by William Virgil Davis. First appeared in *The Davidson Miscellany*.

Alma Denny. "I Love Every Hair Off Your Head": © 1985 by Alma Denny. First appeared in *Cosmopolitan*.

Peter De Vries. "To His Importunate Mistress": Reprinted by permission; © 1986 by Peter De Vries. Originally in *The New Yorker*.

Rochelle Distelheim. "No Muse Is Good Muse": © 1973 by Rochelle Distelheim. First appeared in *McCall's*.

Gavin Ewart. "The Achievements of Herrings": © 1986 by Gavin Ewart. Reprinted from *The Learned Hippopotamus*, Century Hutchinson Ltd. (U.K.).

Robert N. Feinstein. "The TV Chef": © by Robert N. Feinstein. First appeared in *Wisconsin Restauranteur*. "The Fair Fowl": © 1985 by Robert N. Feinstein. First appeared in *Plains Poetry Journal*. "The Court Rests": © 1986 by Robert N. Feinstein. First appeared in *Portland Review*.

F. Scott Fitzgerald. "The Boy Who Killed His Mother": © by F. Scott Fitzgerald. Reprinted from *Neurotica* #9.

Robert Francis. "The Pumpkin Man," "Light and Shadow," and "Where to Spend the Winter": © 1985 by Paul W. Carman. Reprinted from *Butter Hill and Other Poems* (Paul W. Carman, Suite 211, 110 Maple St., Springfield, MA 01105). The first two first appeared in *The Massachusetts Review*.

Jim Hall. "Maybe Dats Youwr Pwoblem Too": © 1980 by Jim Hall. Reprinted from *The Mating Reflex*, Carnegie-Mellon University Press. "Preposterous": © 1985 by Jim Hall. First appeared in *Georgia Review*.

Tom Hansen. "My Lawn Is Brown . . .": © by Tom Hansen. First appeared in *The Archer*.

Mary Jean Irion. "At the Briefing for Creation Day": © 1976 by Mary Jean Irion. First appeared in *The Christian Century*.

Pyke Johnson, Jr. "Gas Man" and "The Man Who Loved a Giraffe": © 1985 and 1986 by Pyke Johnson, Jr. Both first appeared in *Greenwich Time*.

Weldon Kees. "A French Writer Named Sartre" and "Mitzi,": © 1985 by the Estate of Weldon Kees. Reprinted from *Limericks to Friends* (selected by James Reidel, printed by Jordan Davies).

Ron Koertge. "Diary Cows": © by Ron Koertge. Reprinted from *Diary Cows*, Little Caesar Press. " 'These Students Couldn't Write Their Way Out of a Paper Bag' ": © by Ron Koertge. Reprinted from *Life on the Edge of the Continent*, University of Arkansas Press.

David Lehman. "Wystan Hugh Auden: a Villanelle": © 1984 by David Lehman. First appeared in *Shenandoah*.

Kurt Lipschutz. "The Errand Boy's Day Off": © 1985 by Kurt Lipschutz.

Elaine Magarrell. "Loosestrife": © 1985 by Elaine Magarrell. First appeared in *On Hogback Mountain*, Washington Writers' Publishing House.

Gloria A. Maxson. "Worshiper": © 1971 by Gloria A. Maxson. First appeared in *The Christian Century*. "Dentist" and "Decorator" (in "Elegies in a City Churchyard"): © 1984 and 1985 by Gloria A. Maxson. Both first appeared in *National Review*.

Bob McKenty. "The Lamb" and "The Zebra": © 1985 by Bob McKenty. Reprinted from *An AlphaBestiary*.

Lillian Morrison. "Sailing, Sailing": © 1977 by Lillian Morrison. Reprinted from *The Sidewalk Racer*.

Howard Nemerov. "Night Operations, Coastal Command RAF": © 1986 by Howard Nemerov. First appeared in *The Paris Review*.

Ed Ochester. "The Latin American Solidarity Committee Fundraising Picnic": © by Ed Ochester. First appeared in *New Letters*.

Laurence Perrine. "On a Deceased Office-Seeker": © 1977 by Laurence Perrine. First appeared in *The New Laurel Review*. "On a Late Schoolboy": © 1972 by Laurence Perrine. First appeared in *English Journal*.

Marge Piercy. "Arles, 7 p.m.": © 1985 by Marge Piercy.

Elisavietta Ritchie. "Elegy for the Other Woman": © by Elisavietta Ritchie. First appeared in *New York Quarterly*. "Challenges": © 1985 by Elisavietta Ritchie. Reprinted from *The Problem with Eden*, Armstrong State College Press..

Alexis Rotella. "Haiku": © 1985 by Alexis Rotella. Reprinted from *Rearranging Light*, Muse Pie Press..

Hilary Russell. "The Day Willis Harder Didn't Kill His Beagle": © 1983 by Hilary Russell. First appeared in *Hollow Spring Review*. "Earlene Spratt's Lot": © 1983 by Hilary Russell. First appeared in *Yarrow*.

Roberta Simone. "Clerihew Couples" and "A Literary History of Cheese": © 1985 by Roberta Simone.

Knute Skinner. "A Social Engagement": © 1970 by Knute Skinner. First appeared in *Sumac*. "Bailey": © 1985 by Knute Skinner. First appeared in *The Poetry Review*. "The Obligation": © 1974 by Knute Skinner. First appeared in *Poetry Now*. "The Girl Next Door": © 1985 by Knute Skinner. From *Selected Poems* by Knute Skinner, Aquila Press, Scotland (distributed by The Signpost Press, 412 N. State St., Bellingham, WA 98225).

W. D. Snodgrass. "W. D., Don't Fear That Animal" and "Credo": © 1985 by W. D. Snodgrass. First appeared in *Negative Capability*. "Interrogation": © 1985 by W. D. Snodgrass. First appeared in *Salmagundi*.

William Stafford. "Faux Pas": © 1986 by William Stafford. First appeared in *Calapooya Collage*.

Robert D. Sutherland. "The Wonderful World": © 1985 by Robert D. Sutherland.

D. Scott Taylor. "Living Alone": © 1985 by D. Scott Taylor. First appeared in *Rolling Stone*.

Mark Thalman. "The Ants": © 1981 by Mark Thalman. First appeared in *Snapdragon*.

William Trowbridge. "Self Help" and "Viet Kong": © 1986 by William Trowbridge. First appeared in *Poet & Critic*.

Memye Curtis Tucker. "Airport Phone Booth": © 1984 by Memye Curtis Tucker. First appeared in *Southern Humanities Review*.

Lewis Turco. "The Gift": © 1981 by Lewis Turco. First appeared in *Barnwood*. "The Naked Eye": © 1983 by Lewis Turco. First appeared in *Sewanee Review*. "Amherst Neighbors": © 1985 by Lewis Turco. First appeared in *Ontario Review*.

John Updike. "The Sometime Sportsman Greets the Spring": © 1986 by John Updike. First appeared in *The New York Times Sports Magazine*.

Joan Van Poznak. "Love Portions," "Viola D'Amore," and "On Seeing Gavin Ewart in Sainsbury's": © 1983 by Joan Van Poznak. First appeared in *She* (U.K.)..

Irene Warsaw. "Sheep That Pass in the Night": © 1985 by Irene Warsaw. First appeared in *Peninsula Poets*, Poetry Society of Michigan.

Reed Whittemore. "In Memory of an English Professor": © 1948 by Reed Whittemore. First appeared in *MS.*, Carleton College..

L. L. Zeiger. "Envoi": © by L. L. Zeiger. First appeared in *Paris Review* #60.

INDEX OF POETS